GUITAR LICKS
of the
BRIT-ROCK HEROES

By Jesse Gress

Backbeat
Books
San Francisco

Published by Backbeat Books
600 Harrison Street, San Francisco, CA 94107
www.backbeatbooks.com
email: books@musicplayer.com

An imprint of CMP Information
Publishers of *Guitar Player*, *Bass Player*, *Keyboard*, and *EQ* magazines

CMP
United Business Media

Distributed to the book trade in the US and Canada by
Publishers Group West, 1700 Fourth Street, Berkeley, CA 94710

Distributed to the music trade in the US and Canada by
Hal Leonard Publishing, P.O. Box 13819, Milwaukee, WI 53213

Text Design and Composition by Chris Ledgerwood
Cover Design by Richard Leeds — BigWigDesign.com
Front Cover Photo by Robert Knight

Printed in the United States of America

04 05 06 07 08   5 4 3 2 1

Dedicated to my father,
Dr. Francis A. Gress,
and
in memory of
James "Otis" Nastasee

CONTENTS

INTRODUCTION

IMPROVISING MUSICIANS—or "spontaneous reorganizers," as I like to call them—are limited only by the scope of their musical vocabulary, which includes not only licks and musical ideas, but also the ability to manipulate them in a wide variety of contexts. One way to enhance your musical vocabulary is to emulate your favorite players, and, as most accomplished improvisers will tell you, the best way to understand how your favorite musicians play is to get inside their heads by studying their licks and analyzing their styles. When you listen to and analyze a large cross-section of any musician's work, certain phrases and techniques will inevitably surface as recurring motifs in their improvisations. It is these elements of repetition and spontaneous reorganization—plus the framework in which they are presented—that form the basis of a musician's style.

Omnipotent guitarists Eric Clapton, Jeff Beck, and Jimmy Page have amassed huge musical vocabularies. But while all three share similar backgrounds and influences, use essentially the same tools, and are inexorably linked by their collective Yardbirds heritage, each has developed an immediately identifiable and highly personalized style. In this series, we'll travel into the minds and motor systems of this royal trinity of British rock guitar by taking licks fashioned from each player's musical vocabulary and applying them to a variety of familiar accompaniment grooves and harmonic settings. This first volume traces their development from the mid '60s through the mid '70s, a particularly fertile and influential period in each player's four-decade career.

Besides acting as building blocks in your own improvisational arsenal, these licks will offer important insights when you analyze the recordings of Clapton, Beck, and Page. The licks are organized into various categories of accompaniment grooves, such as medium and fast shuffles, straight-eighth and funky 16th-note rock, and slow blues. At the beginning of each groove, you'll find an explanatory page that defines the key, tempo, and feel; suggests accompaniment patterns and chord fingerings; and offers helpful tips and guidelines that apply to all examples using that groove. (The appendix lists the scales and modes used in each groove.) The Recommended Listening recordings serve as a basic guide to the essence of each groove. You're highly encouraged (wink, wink) to check out live recordings of these players.

On the CD I demonstrate each lick. The example numbers correspond with the track numbers, and each multi-part example appears on its own track. (To accommodate this convenience, the tuning reference is located on Track 99.) An unobtrusive bass drum and hi-hat pulse set at the lowest suggested tempo accompanies each lick. Preceding each example, you'll hear a one-bar count; if the lick begins with a pickup, you'll hear a two-bar count. Use the few seconds of silence before the count-off to get your bearings. To hear the original intention of each lick, record your own backing track based on the suggested accompaniment figure described at the beginning of each groove, and then play along. This way you can work at your own speed and gradually increase the tempo at a comfortable rate. Once you own a lick, transpose it to as many keys as possible and experiment with using it in various contexts.

So—why these guys? Well, they're my heroes. Let's just say that all three sent my 12-year-old world spinning, and I've been a fan(atic) ever since. Ready to jump in? Join me now as we delve deep to reveal the secrets behind the licks of rock guitar's founding fathers.

GUIDE TO NOTATIONAL SYMBOLS

THE FOLLOWING SYMBOLS are used in *Guitar Lick Factory* to notate fingerings, techniques, and effects commonly used in guitar music. Certain symbols are found in either the tablature or the standard notation only, not both. For clarity, consult both systems.

4● : Left-hand fingering is designated by small Arabic numerals near note heads (1=first finger, 2=middle finger, 3=third finger, 4=little finger, t=thumb).

p● : Right-hand fingering designated by letters (p=thumb, i=first finger, m=middle finger, a=third finger, c=little finger).

②● : A circled number (1–6) indicates the string on which a note is to be played.

⊓ : Pick downstroke.

Ⅴ : Pick upstroke.

Bend: Play the first note and bend to the pitch of the equivalent fret position shown in parentheses.

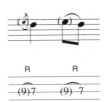

Reverse Bend: Prebend the note to the specified pitch/fret position shown in parentheses. Play, then release to indicated pitch/fret.

Hammer-on: From lower to higher note(s). Individual notes may also be hammered.

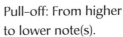

Pull-off: From higher to lower note(s).

Slide: Play first note and slide up or down to the next pitch. If the notes are tied, pick only the first. If no tie is present, pick both.

A slide symbol before or after a single note indicates a slide to or from an undetermined pitch.

Finger vibrato.

Bar vibrato.

Bar dips, dives, and bends: Numerals and fractions indicate distance of bar bends in half-steps.

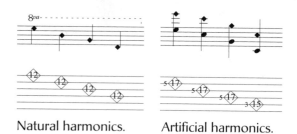

Natural harmonics.   Artificial harmonics.

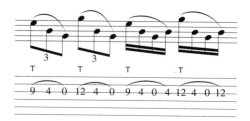

Pick-hand tapping: Notes are hammered with a pick-hand finger, usually followed by additional hammer-ons and pull-offs.

Trill.

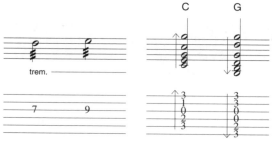

Tremolo picking.   Strum: Arrow heads indicate direction.

HOW TABLATURE WORKS

The horizontal lines represent the guitar's strings, the top line standing for the high *E*. The numbers designate the frets to be played. For instance, a 2 positioned on the first line would mean play the 2nd fret on the first string (0 indicates an open string). Time values are indicated on the standard notation staff seen directly above the tablature. Special symbols and instructions appear between the standard and tablature staves.

CHORD DIAGRAMS

In all chord diagrams, vertical lines represent the strings, and horizontal lines represent the frets. The following symbols are used:

————— Nut; indicates first position.

X Muted string, or string not played.

○ Open string.

⌒ Barre (partial or full).

● Placement of left-hand fingers.

III Roman numerals indicate the fret at which a chord is located.

Arabic numerals indicate left-hand fingering.

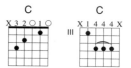

ERIC CLAPTON

PRIOR TO EMERGING as the first bona fide British guitar hero, Eric Clapton was a young blues fanatic who spent his time absorbing the music of Muddy Waters, Howlin' Wolf, B.B. King, Albert King, Freddie King, Buddy Guy, Otis Rush, and other blues greats. Researching the prewar influences of these players led him to Blind Blake, Blind Willie Johnson, and, ultimately, Robert Johnson.

An original member of the Yardbirds, Clapton left the group in 1965 due to differences in musical direction—he was a blues purist but his bandmates were heading into pop territory. When EC joined John Mayall's Bluesbreakers in 1966, he set the course for the future of blues and rock guitar. His innovative soloing on *Blues Breakers: John Mayall with Eric Clapton* merged his stylistic influences with a fat, sustained tone that was unprecedented and absolutely electrifying. The album remains essential listening for all guitarists.

With the formation of Cream—rock's first supergroup—Clapton and cohorts Jack Bruce and Ginger Baker blazed a trail that defined the heavy power trio format and created a model for hundreds of bands to follow. In addition to innovative original material, Cream's albums *Fresh Cream*, *Disraeli Gears*, *Wheels of Fire*, and *Goodbye* introduced the music of Muddy Waters, Robert Johnson, Skip James, and Willie Dixon to a massive new audience via high-octane versions of "Rollin' and Tumblin'" (Waters), "Crossroads" (Johnson), "I'm So Glad" (James), and "Spoonful" (Dixon). When the band performed live, the jams often stretched for 20 minutes or more, with group improvisation featuring the kind of collective interplay previously found only in jazz ensembles. Cream's mass acceptance soon led to a public craving for extended guitar solos—previously unheard of, but a harbinger of things to come.

When Cream imploded in 1969, EC went on to form the short-lived but acclaimed Blind Faith with Steve Winwood and Ginger Baker, and Derek & the Dominos, whose *Layla and Other Assorted Love Songs* became an instant classic. Since then, Clapton has enjoyed tremendous success as a solo artist, often working in other genres but never straying far from his blues roots.

A Fender convert since 1970 (Clapton now has his own signature series Fender Stratocaster), EC was a Gibson man during most of the period represented in this book, favoring Les Pauls, Les Paul/SGs, ES–335s, and Firebirds cranked through 50-watt and 100-watt Marshall stacks. Except for occasionally employing a wah-wah pedal, Clapton sculpted his sound—from aggressive razor-sharp treble-pickup bite to the subtle delicacy of his famous neck-pickup/highs-rolled-off "woman tone"—using only his guitar, his amp, and, most important, his hands. Arguably the smoothest and cleanest player of our three Brit-rock heroes, Clapton may also be the most repetitious, but certainly not in a bad way: EC had a lot of space to fill during Cream's lengthy jams, and though he constantly recycled and recast many of the same basic ideas, they never sound tiresome or redundant.

The following 40 EC-style licks fall into seven accompaniment categories, or grooves. As you dig in, keep in mind that Clapton's concise sense of rhythm, elegant phrasing, resonant microtonal bends, fiery upper-register triplets, and fluid vibrato are all key elements of his style. Practice them until they sound fit for royalty.

ERIC CLAPTON–Style Licks

Groove #1
Fast blues shuffle with swing feel.

Key: G   **Tempo:** ♩ = 180–204

Suggested accompaniment: 12-bar "slow-change" blues progression with a static I-chord turnaround in bars 11 and 12. (Slow-change refers to 12-bar blues progressions in which the IV chord does not appear until bar 5, i.e. I–I–I–I–IV–IV–I–I–V–V–I–I, played for one bar each.) Graft the following single-note shapes to the illustrated rhythm and navigate the root–octave–♭7–5 riff through each I, IV, and V chord (*G7, C7, D7*), or comp freely on the suggested chord voicings.

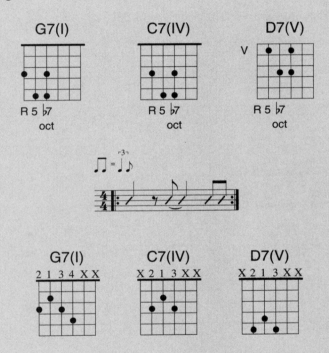

Tips: Though a definite swing feel is present, adjacent eighth-notes played at this tempo often breeze by as straight, not swung, eighths. Three-note subdivisions of the beat tend to shift between eighth-note triplets and combined eighth- and 16th-note figures. Melodically, these licks are based on the "box" positions formed here by the G pentatonic minor scale, G pentatonic major scale, and G blues scale. For reference, the numbered position of a pentatonic or blues box is determined by the location of your 1st finger on the fretboard.

Recommended listening: Cream, "Stepping Out" on *Live Cream, Vol. 2* (Universal); John Mayall's Bluesbreakers, *Blues Breakers: John Mayall with Eric Clapton* (Deram); and on various Clapton and Cream collections.

Example 1 kicks off a 12-bar chorus. Purely *G* pentatonic minor, the first three bars slip from third to sixth position and back again, and illustrate many techniques inherent in Clapton's style. Following a two-note pickup, we opt for a slide rather than a bend to the 5 (*D*). Play this grace slide with your 2nd finger—this sets you up to play the sixth-position notes in bar 2 and return to third position in bar 3. (You'll be seeing a lot of this move.) Be sure to observe the sweet vibrato, staccato notes, resonant microtonal bends, and other emotive phrasing techniques present throughout these examples.

The remaining four bars jump to 11th position and remain anchored there for a ride through the IV chord (*C7*). Plant your 3rd finger at the 13th fret and 1st finger in 11th position and you're good to go. (Hint: Grab the high *F* at the end of bar 5 with your 4th finger.) In bar 7, you'll find one non-pentatonic note, *F#*, or the 7, which Clapton often used as a passing tone. Play Ex. 1 over bars 1–7 of the 12-bar slow-change form.

Ex. 1

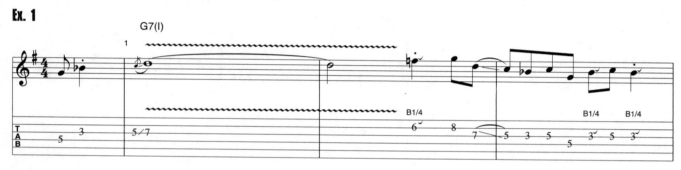

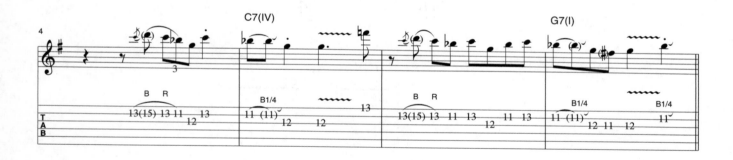

Example 2's out-of-the-ordinary bend to the 6 (*E*) is held and syncopated in the alternative 13th-position move. Notice how this note is transformed from the 6 of *G* to the 3 of *C* as we cross the bar line into IV–chord territory. True to the Clapton style, the unusual conclusion to this lick dances between *G* pentatonic major and *G* pentatonic minor tonalities. Play Ex. 2 over bars 4–7 of the 12-bar form.

Ex. 2

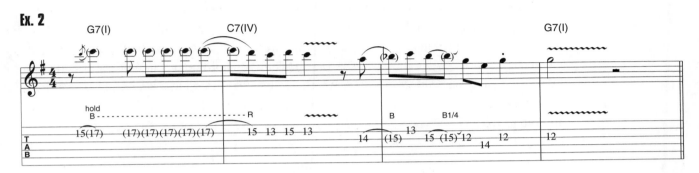

Example 3 begins with a third-position Clapton staple—a pull-off from ♭7 to 5 (*F* to *D*) followed by the 4 and 5 (*C* and *D*), a slightly bent ♭3 (*B♭*), a pull-off from the root to the ♭7 (*G* to *F*), and a target root on the downbeat of bar 2. Again, use your 2nd finger to slide up to the 7th fret and remain in sixth position (1st finger at the 6th fret and 3rd finger at the 8th fret) to cover the V chord (*D7*) riffage in bar 3. (Note that the last note of the lick drops to fifth position.) The root-9 bend and release, a cheesy-sounding move over the I and IV chords, is perfectly placed here, where it functions as an in-the-pocket motif over *D7*. Play Ex. 3 over bars 7–9 of the 12-bar form.

Ex. 3

Example 4 — You'll find another EC trademark in the first two measures of Ex. 4, our first excursion into eighth position. Begin with your 1st finger planted on the *B*-string at the 8th fret, grab the 11th-fret *B♭*, bend a whole-step to *C* on beat *one*, and gradually rebend the same note a half-step on beat *two*. Continue with the root–6–root move (*G–E–G*) on beats *two* and *three*, then bend *A* to *B* with your 3rd finger and hold it while you fret the 10th-fret *D* with your 4th finger. Sting and shake the root and slide off it, and you've nailed the tasty blend of major and minor pentatonicisms in the first phrase.

Sounding more than a bit Beck-ish, the second phrase (bars 3 and 4) drops down to the third-position *G* pentatonic box and features multiple quarter-step bends on the *♭3s* (*B♭*) and a cool, almost imperceptible prebend to the 5 (*D*). The 11th-position IV-chord run in bar 5 borrows its rhythm from bar 3. In true call-and-response tradition, this motif is repeated beginning on an eighth-note upbeat and elongated in bar 6, where you'll find the return of Clapton's signature *F#* passing tone. The smooth moves in bars 7 and 8 bring the lick to a close over the I chord. Play Ex. 4 over bars 1–8 of the 12-bar slow-change progression.

Ex. 4

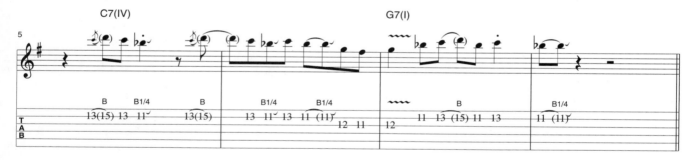

Example 5 — Derived entirely from the ever-popular 15th-position *G* pentatonic minor blues box, Ex. 5 depicts a plethora of upper-register Clapton-isms. Bar 1's opening phrase recaps the second half of bar 1 in Ex. 3 one octave higher, and then continues with an anticipated oblique unison bend in which one *G* remains stationary while the other is bent. The bend–release–pull-off maneuver in the middle of bar 2 is a typical EC move, as are the adjacent whole- and quarter-step bends played over the IV chord in bar 3.

The remainder of this example utilizes a repetitive two-beat motif consisting of a quarter-note bend to the root followed by a descending eighth-note triplet (root–♭7–5). Clapton was perhaps the first rock guitarist to popularize this type of repetitive high-octane riffing. The momentum this lick produces is so powerful you could actually ride it through the entire 12-bar progression. Play Ex. 5 over bars 3–8 of the 12-bar form.

Ex. 5

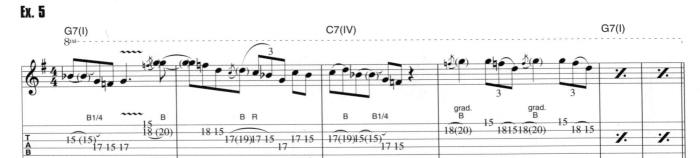

Example 6 — tabbed with an alternative fingering—shows how EC takes a short motif that spans one-and-a-half beats (three eighth-notes) and rhythmically displaces it over three measures until it recycles. The official term for this type of three-against-four rhythmic displacement is *hemiola*. Think of it as subdividing three bars of 4/4 into eight bars of 3/8 within the same time frame.

In this case, the 3/8 motif consists of two eighth-notes—bent and stationary 5s (*D*)—followed by two 16th-notes—the ♭7 (*F*) pulled off to the 5 (*D*). Check out how this motif repeats every one-and-a-half beats, or three eighth-notes. This example begins with a pickup on beat *four*, but the lick works equally well starting on any eighth-note downbeat or upbeat. Play Ex. 6 over any part of the 12-bar progression.

Ex. 6

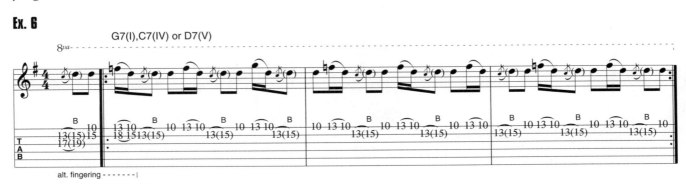

Example 7 shows how Clapton might adapt the same rhythm to a different set of notes over a V–IV–I progression (*D7– C7– G7*). This repetitive sixth-position 5–♭7–root–v7 motif (*D–F–G–F*) functions as the root–♭3–4–♭3 of *D7*, and the 2–4–5–4 of *C7*. Notice how the 3/8 hemiola is broken off after its fifth repetition—one-and-a-quarter measures before it fully recycles. Play Ex. 7 into and over bars 9–11 of the 12-bar form.

Ex. 7

Example 8 — In Ex. 8, the rhythm of the previous 3/8 hemiola is reordered into an eighth–16th–16th–eighth motif. Here, a 15th-position ♭7–♭3 double-stop (*F* and *B♭*) begins each 3/8 repetition, followed by pulled-off root–♭7 16th-notes (*G–F*) and an eighth-note 5 (*D*). Like Ex. 6, this lick takes three bars to recycle. Play Ex. 8 over any part of the 12-bar progression.

Ex. 8

Example 9 illustrates how EC incorporates repetitive rhythmic displacements like the ones in Examples 6–8 into the fabric of his improvisations. Once again, we're locked into the 15th-position *G* pentatonic minor blues box throughout. The opening phrase begins with a three-note Chuck Berry–style run on beat *two*. (EC refined this move early in his career and has since taken it beyond Berry's wildest dreams.) Anticipate the ♭7–root bend on the *and* of beat *four*, then complete bar 2's swinging signature bend–release–pull-off maneuver. Bar 3 mixes up the 4, ♭3, and 5, while bar 4 begins with a sweet anticipated bend to the 6 (*E*) and drops to the 4 (*C*) before concluding with a simple reverse *G* minor arpeggio. It's amazing how Clapton can inject such soul and emotion into something as simple as a common three-note arpeggio.

Bar 5, the change to the IV chord (*C7*), picks up the pace beginning with a repetitive 3/8 ride on *D*, which functions here as the 9 of *C7*. Halfway through bar 6 the 3/8 hemiola morphs into the same one shown in Ex. 6. Play Ex. 9 over bars 1–8 of the 12-bar slow-change progression.

Ex. 9

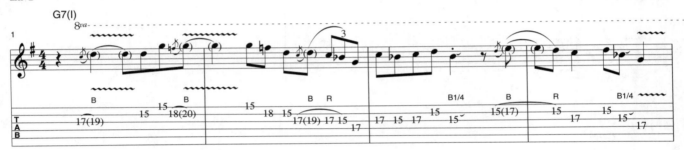

Example 10 and 11 — Clapton gets a lot of mileage out of his licks by adapting the same rhythms to different notes. Played over the IV–I change, the first two bars of Ex. 10 and Ex. 11 are identical rhythmically, but are composed of different raw melodic materials. Both adapt the previous 3/8 rhythmic displacements to single dotted-eighth-note hits. Example 10 features oblique bends utilizing the 5 and ♭7 (functioning as 9 and 11 over *C7*), while Ex. 11 superimposes a wide root–♭3 bend (5–♭7 over *C7*) onto the same rhythm. Notice how the last bend in both examples is held and then given a grace-note release.

Check out the return of the *F#* passing tone in Ex. 10 and the recurrence of those familiar sixth-to-third-to-sixth-position slides in Ex. 11. Both examples cover bars 5–7, but Ex. 10 is elongated to include bar 8 and the V-chord change in bar 9.

Ex. 10

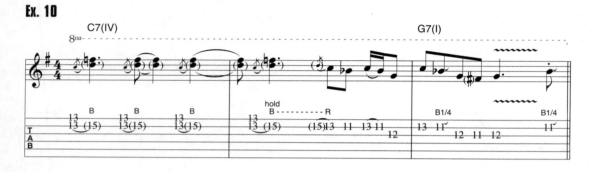

Ex. 11

Example 12 shows how to string together many of the EC-style moves we've seen so far—plus a few new ones—into a complete 12-bar solo chorus played entirely in the third and sixth positions. The four-note pickup is notable for its inclusion of the 6 (*E*), and you'll find the first three bars to be a variation on Ex. 1.

In the second phrase, beginning on beat *two* of bar 4, we play into and out of the IV chord (*C7*) using a few familiar moves, some revamped with slight phrasing alterations. The V- and IV-chord licks in bars 9 and 10 are spin-offs of bars 6 and 5, in that order. Look closely and you'll notice that the eight-note lick starting on the downbeat of bar 5 is virtually identical to the one that starts on beat *four* of bar 9. Bars 11 and 12 wrap things up with slinky bends and hammered double-stops. Play Ex. 12 over the entire 12-bar slow-change blues progression (bars 1–12).

Ex. 12

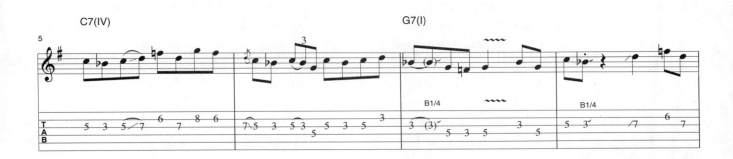

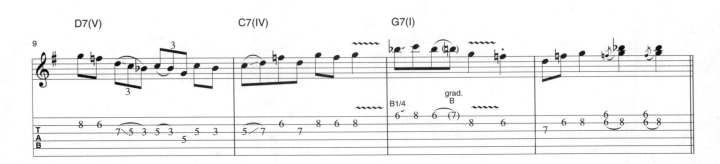

Example 13 begins with some familiar sixth- and third-position moves, but check out the twist in bar 3; we've taken the repetitive motif from bars 4–6 of Ex. 5 (minus the gradual bend) and stretched the quarter-notes into half-notes to create a 3/4 hemiola. In other words, we use three quarter-notes rather than three eighth-notes to rhythmically displace the lick at half the speed of a 3/8 hemiola. Picture it as the subdivision of three bars of 4/4 into four bars of 3/4. Play Ex. 13 over bars 1–5 of the 12-bar slow-change progression. (Hint: Try keeping the 3/4 hemiola going over the remaining seven bars.)

Ex. 13

Example 14 also covers the I and IV chords (*G7–C7*), beginning with a 3/8 hemiola that morphs into an adaptation of the displaced licks from Examples 6 and 7. Starting this three-note motif on beat *four* of the previous measure sets up a perfect segue to the embellished four-note displacement in bars 3 and 4. The 10th-position note choices here—the 6, 5, and ♭3—sound particularly bittersweet in this configuration. The shape formed by these notes on the 1st and 2nd strings is the same as the one you've used to play many 11th-position licks on the 2nd and 3rd strings. (This is another hemiola that can be driven across the entire 12-bar progression.) Drop into eighth position to cover the IV chord and be sure to hold the bend in bar 6 rock steady until its release on the "and" of beat *three*. Play Ex. 14 over bars 1–7 of the 12-bar slow-change progression.

Ex. 14

Example 15 and 16 — The four-bar I-chord quickies in Ex. 15 and Ex. 16 prove there are few, if any, limitations to how these basic blues elements may be rearranged. For instance, check out the first two beats in bar 1 of Ex. 15; we've seen several rhythmic variations of this two-beat bend–release–pull-off motif several times before—starting on beat *two* in bar 2 of Ex. 5 and bar 4 of Ex. 12, and on beat *three* in bar 2 of Ex. 9—but never starting on beat *one*, as it does here. Watch for it to show up on beat *four*.

Example 16 begins with a syncopated bend to the 5 (*D*) held beneath the b7 (*F*) and grace-note-released back to the 4 (*C*). The transition to bar 2 features a new set of moves; a fragment of a descending IV-chord arpeggio on beat *four* of bar 1 is paired with a reverse *G* minor arpeggio played as a quarter-note triplet and followed up with another b7–root–b3 triplet. (Remember, that quarter-step bend is crucial.)

After a beat of rest in bar 3, a piercing high *G* wails for two beats, then gives way to a descending root–b7–5 (*G–F–D*) eighth-note triplet. (Recognize this move from Ex. 13?) And lo and behold, the second half of the final phrase (bar 4) reverses the first two notes of the motif from Examples 5 and 9, which were examined in Ex. 15. Play Ex. 15 and Ex. 16 over bars 1–4 of the 12-bar slow-change progression

Ex. 15

Ex. 16

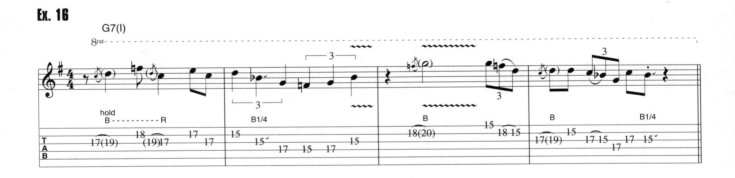

Example 17 — We'll wrap up this fast blues shuffle groove back in 15th position. Clapton may have never realized he was hammering into a *Bb/D* arpeggio with the 3 in the bass when he laid down licks like the one that opens Ex. 17, but that's exactly what he was doing. All of the remaining action in bars 1–3 takes place on the 3rd and 4th strings using only two notes per string. The lovely half-note bend to the 5 (*D*) in bar 3 provides a breather before the stinging 5–b7–5 (*D–F–D*) hammer-pull triplet combo in bar 4. Observe the staccato phrasing on the *C* that follows on beat *four*—it makes this signature EC lick come to life. You can also repeat and displace this two-beat motif as we did in Examples 5 and 13.

Begin Ex. 17 at bar 9 and play through bar 12 into bar 1 of the following chorus. Of course, like most of these licks, you can plop them into any part of the 12-bar slow-change progression and they'll work just fine.

Ex. 17

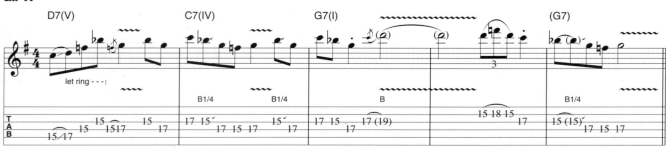

Groove #2   Medium blues shuffle.

Key: *A*   **Tempo:** ♩ = 112–136

Suggested accompaniment: 12-bar "quick-change" blues progression with a I–V turnaround (*G7–D7*) in bars 11 and 12. ("Quick-change" refers to 12-bar blues progressions where the IV chord replaces the I chord in bar 2, i.e. I–IV–I–I–IV–IV–I–I–V–V–I–V, played for one bar each.) Play two swung eighth-notes per chord on the Chicago-style root–5 and root–6 voicings shown below, adapting them to the I, IV, and V chords (*A, D,* and *E*) as you go. Alternatively, you can comp freely on the illustrated *A7, D7,* and *E7* shapes.

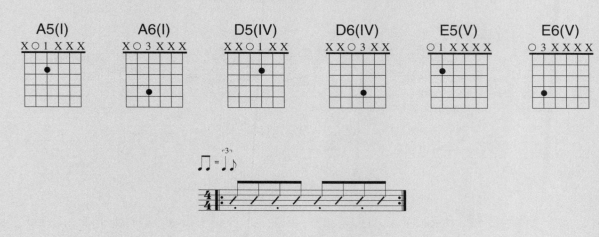

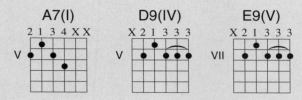

Tips: At this moderate tempo, it's natural and comfortable to swing those paired eighth-notes, and all three-note groupings are played as eighth-note triplets.

Recommended listening: Cream, "Lawdy Mama" on *Live Cream, Vol. 1* (Universal).

Example 18 — Short and sweet, Ex. 18 hangs on a repetitive eighth-note triplet motif in fifth position—a quick bend from ♭3 to 3 (*C* to *C#*) followed by a descending root and 5 (*A* and *E*)—for seven beats before breaking the tension with a now-familiar 4–5–♭3–root run (*D–E–C–A*). The half-step bend blurs the distinction between major and minor tonalities—a good thing in the blues.

Play Ex. 18 anywhere between bars 1 and 4 or in bars 7–9 of the 12-bar "quick-change" progression. Though the *C#* is technically a "wrong" note for *D7*, sheer momentum will allow you to plow this triplet through all three chord changes.

Ex. 19

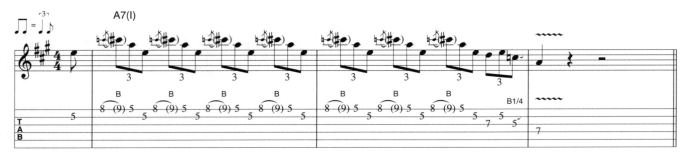

Example 19 — Another quickie, Ex. 19 derives its repetitive twin-triplet lick from the second-position *A* pentatonic major scale. Repeat the six-note motif three times, then top it off with the variation in the second half of bar 2.

Example 19 works best over the I chord (*A7*), but again, you can try it on bars 3–5 or 7–9.

Ex. 19

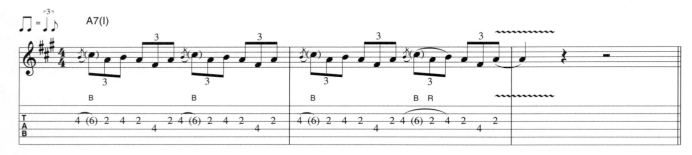

Example 20 — Played over the I chord, Ex. 20 begins with a ♭3–3–5–root climb (*C–C♯–E–A*), and then echoes Ex. 18's triplet motif using swung eighth-notes. An extended reverse *A* minor arpeggio (*E–C–A–E*) that includes a 5 played below the root highlights the V chord (*E7*) in bar 2.

The frantic *C–C♯* half-step bends in bar 3 (again, "wrong" for the IV, or *D7*, chord) create a propulsive two-against-three polyrhythm—a reverse hemiola, if you will! The I–V turnaround in bars 4 and 5 dances around five familiar scale tones—*A, C, C♯, D,* and *E*—and still manages to smell fresh as a daisy. Play Ex. 20 over bars 8–12 of the 12-bar form.

Ex. 20

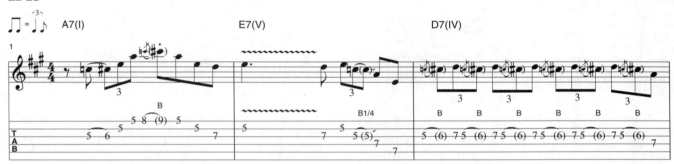

Groove #3

Medium-tempo psychedelic blues/rock.

Key: D   **Tempo:** ♩ = 96–106

Suggested accompaniment: Play the illustrated *D5*, *G5/C*, *G/B*, and *B♭* voicings as driving four-on-the-floor quarter-notes for two beats each. Go for a warm and fuzzy "brown" sound. In some examples, every other measure ends with *B♭* and *C*, each played for a single beat.

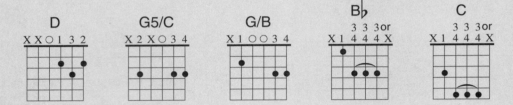

Tips: These examples reflect the type of groundbreaking licks Clapton used to fuel Cream's extended psychedelic blues/rock excursions over non-blues chord progressions. The rhythmic emphasis here is on quarter-, eighth-, and 16th-notes, plus the occasional 16th-note triplet. Break out your wah-wah pedal and begin by rocking heel-to-toe quarter-notes, and you'll soon get the hang of tone-sculpting these licks any way you desire.

Recommended listening: Cream, "Tales of Brave Ulysses" on *Disraeli Gears* (Universal) and "White Room" on *Wheels of Fire* (Polydor); both tracks can also be found on various Cream collections.

Example 21 — Locking into the 10th-position *D* pentatonic minor blues box, Ex. 21 superimposes elements of EC's blues vocabulary over a psych/rock progression built on a descending bass line (*D–C–B–B♭*). Check out how this harmony affects each blues lick. Bar 1 begins with a pair of oblique quarter-note bends involving a bent 5 (*A*) and stationary ♭7 (*C*). In contrast, the response in bar 2 injects busier 16th-note rhythms to create momentum. Clapton really likes to keep the ball moving; you've probably noticed by now that there's not a lot of space in any of these licks. Give the *F* half-note in bar 3 a serious shake before finishing up with the remaining flurry of 16th-note activity in bar 4. You should be familiar with most of these moves by now, but you'll be surprised by how different they sound in this new harmonic framework.

Ex. 21

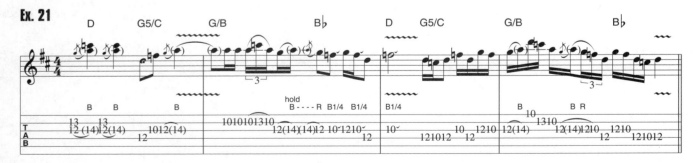

Example 22 — For classic elegance, you can't beat the quarter-, eighth-, and half-note bends that kick off Ex. 22. Once again, the shifting harmonies recast a basic blues move in a completely different light. The second half of bar 2 features a particularly cool sleight-of-hand involving a pair of adjacent *A* notes—one prebent and one unbent—sandwiched between the 4 (*G*) and ♭7 (*C*). Of course, the function of these notes changes relative to the chord of the moment. Bar 3 contains another variation of a move we've seen previously—check out beat *two* in Ex. 21.

Ex. 22

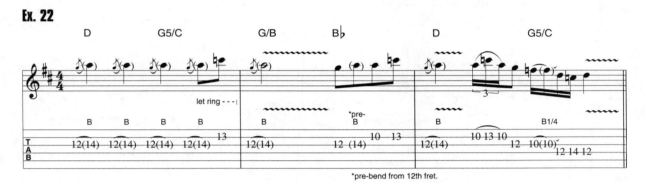

*pre-bend from 12th fret.

Example 23 — The concise, rapid-fire lick in Ex. 23 covers every note of the 10th-position blues box on the bottom five strings before sliding down to eighth position. Most of its elements should have an air of familiarity.

Ex. 23

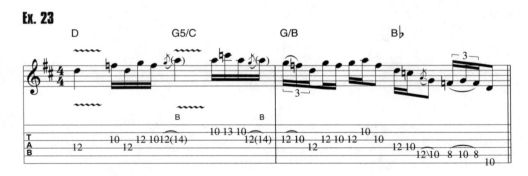

Example 24 — An additional chord is pasted into the progression in Ex. 24 and the remaining examples of this groove—C on beat *four* of every other measure. It's a subtle change, but one that effectively reharmonizes the notes played on that beat. From the opening oblique unison bend to the bend/hammer-on move that crosses from bar 1 to bar 2, you can detect the influence of Jimi Hendrix. The recurring hammer-on on beat *one* of bars 4 and 5 creates a nice sense of development and continuity. You'll also find a couple of oblique double-stop hammer-ons and pull-offs in bar 4. Note how the double-stop on beat *four* is pulled off from a single *D* note.

The whole lick remains locked in the 10th-position *D* blues box and traverses the top five strings.

Ex. 24

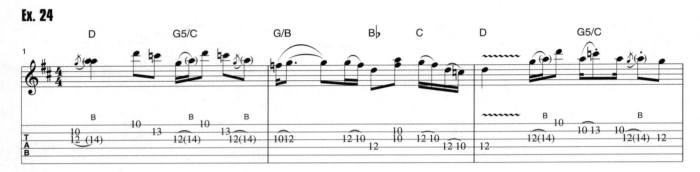

Example 25 — Following an opening four-note pickup that recalls Hendrix's intro to "Hey Joe," the first two measures in Ex. 25 feature perhaps the most syncopation we've seen thus far. Begin the pickup in fifth position, slide down to third position, and remain there until beat *four* of bar 1. Here, we start a series of sliding position shifts on the *D* and *G* strings. The first slide brings us back to fifth position, the next one skips to the *G* string and slips from *D* at the 7th fret to *F* at the 10th fret, and the last shift moves from *F* to *G* at the 12th fret. Play each slide with your third (ring) finger and you'll arrive back in 10th position on the second 16th-note (or "ee") of beat *three*, bar 2.

   That's a lovely lick in itself, but we've tagged on another two bars of 10th-position riffing for good measure. Noteworthy highlights include an exquisitely vibrated bent half-note "breather," ♭7/root and 5/root double-stops, staccato notes, and a flashy hammered-and-pulled 16th-note triplet.

Ex. 25

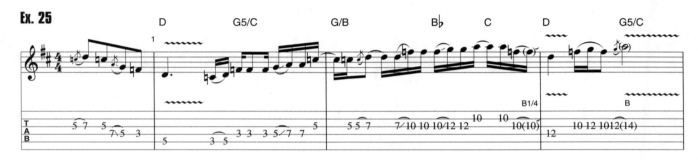

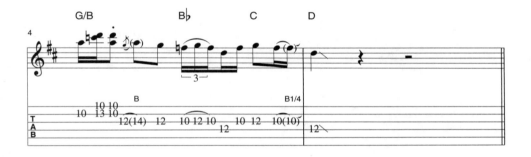

Example 26 — The opening two-beat motif in Ex. 26 (excluding the pickup) is a slippery new move that adapts a descending five-note melodic pattern first to the top three strings and then to the 2nd, 3rd, and 4th strings. Grab the last *G* in bar 1 with your 2nd finger and ride the 3rd-string bus up to the 14th fret. This anchors your 1st finger in 13th position, where you can easily finger the syncopated dyads (two-note chords) in bar 2. Sound the 5 and ♭7 (*A* and *C*) simultaneously on beats *one* and *two*, and then separate them for beats *three* and *four*.

The last note in beat *four* marks a temporary return to 10th position in bar 3. Use the same second-finger slide to zip back up to 13th position, and milk that one-and-a-half-step bend for all it's worth.

Ex. 26

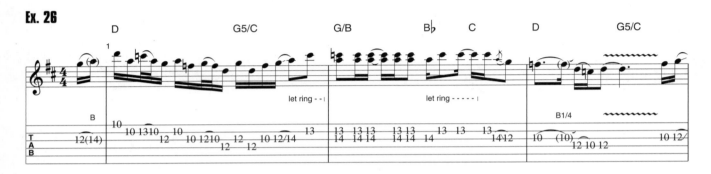

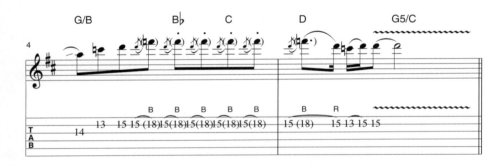

Example 27, our last psychedelic blues/rock lick over this groove, begins in 13th position, roams 10th position, and ends up in eighth position, covering every string along the way. Nail the opening one-and-a-half-step bend with your 3rd finger and you're set up to play most of the next two measures.

Bar 2 starts with a quick 3/16 hemiola and quickly sets up the forthcoming descent to 10th position. You can pick out an *F* triad shape in the first half of beat *three*.

The last two measures utilize every available note of the *D* pentatonic minor scale on all six strings. The final *C* note coincides perfectly with the chord of the moment.

Ex. 27

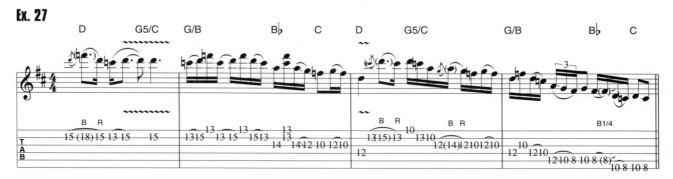

Groove #4

Moderately fast blues-rock with straight eighth-note feel.

Key: *A*   **Tempo**: ♩ = 106–132

Suggested accompaniment: A 12-bar "quick-change" blues progression—with a I-chord turnaround—utilizing the illustrated Chuck Berry–style voicings adapted to the I, IV, and V chords (*A*, *D* and *E*). Alternate between root–5 and root–6 chords, playing each one as two straight eighth-notes per beat.

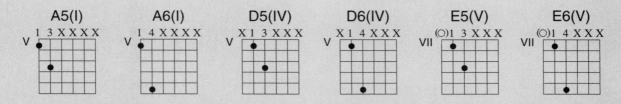

Tips: Again, the rhythmic emphasis in these licks is on straight eighth-notes, 16th-notes, and 16th-note triplets. Cream's take on the Robert Johnson classic "Crossroads" features a signature root–octave–♭7–octave–♭7–octave–♭7 guitar riff (*A–A–G–A–G–A–G*), which appears every other two bars during the "quick-change" verse progression. Their arrangement often switched to a slow-change progression during the extended guitar solo, but the following examples work equally well over both forms. Interestingly, EC rearranged the song for Blind Faith's concert repertoire by reducing the tempo and significantly altering his signature single-note riff.

Recommended listening: Cream, "Crossroads" on *Wheels of Fire* (Polydor) and various Cream collections.

Example 28 captures the rhythmic and melodic essence of Clapton's style during the peak of Cream's popularity circa 1968. We're back in the eighth-position *A* pentatonic minor box for the opening one-and-a-half-step bend from the root to the ♭3, or ♯9 (*C*). You can strengthen this or any 3rd-fingered bend by using your 2nd finger to reinforce it one fret lower. Follow up with the vibrated root on beat *two*, and then slip back and forth from eighth to fifth position for the remainder of bar 1—you know the routine. In bar 2—the "quick change" to the IV chord (*D*)—we stay in the fifth-position *A* pentatonic minor blues box until beat *four* before riding the *G*-string back up to eighth position to greet the I chord.

In bars 3 and 4, we return to eighth position, but this time we use a lick derived from the *A* pentatonic major scale to approach the IV chord. The repeated six-note motif in bar 3 forms a momentary 3/8 hemiola. If you choose to play the sustained *C♯* bends and high *E*'s with your 3rd and 4th fingers, you'll have to switch fingers for the consecutive eighth-note bends and releases in bar 4 (unless you're a 4th-finger bender). You may want to try initiating those *C♯* bends with your 2nd finger and grabbing the *E*'s with your 3rd finger. Play Ex. 28 over bars 1–5 of the 12-bar "quick-change" progression.

Ex. 28

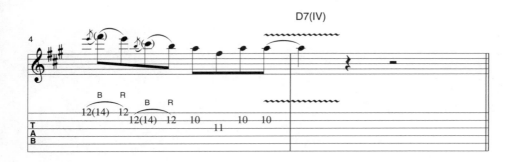

Example 29 covers a sizable chunk of 12-bar real estate. The slip-and-slide moves over the IV chord in bar 1 differ from those we've seen previously. Here, we elongate the phrase by hanging on the *G* for two full beats before sliding into fifth-position blues box territory. The *C–C♯* grace-note hammer-on on the downbeat of bar 3 absolutely nails the return to the I chord, while the open *A* string on beat *four* allows you time to shift down to second position for the *A* pentatonic major moves in bar 4.

Recognize the two-beat bend-and-release maneuver that begins on beat *three* of bar 5? It's identical to the one in bar 4 of Ex. 28, but it's played one octave lower over the V chord (*E*). Remain in second position for the rapid-fire pull-offs in bar 6, and wrap it up with an open-*A* breather. Play Ex. 29 over bars 5–11 of the 12-bar progression.

Ex. 29

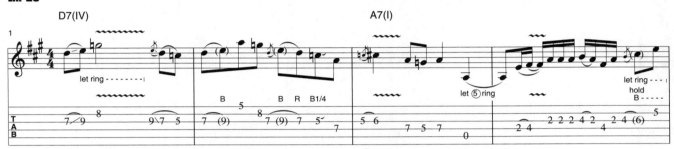

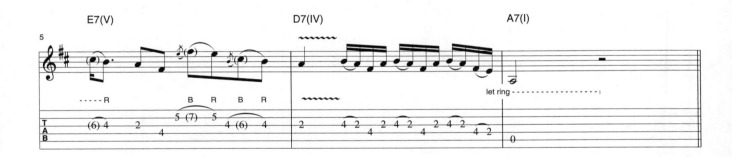

Example 30 shows another 10th-position *A* pentatonic major lick played over two bars of the I chord. This example designates the V chord (*E*) as the point of arrival, but the lick works equally well as an approach to the IV chord (*D*). We end with a snippet from yet another 3/8 hemiola. Play Ex. 30 over bars 7–9 of the 12-bar progression.

Ex. 30

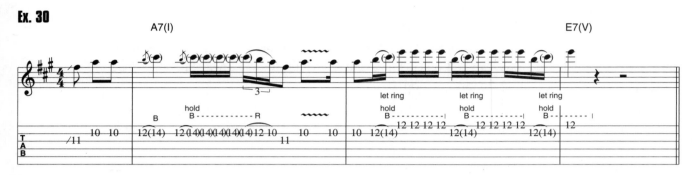

Example 31 depicts the "quick-change" to the IV chord in bar 2 of the 12-bar progression, plus the transitions to the I and V chords. Excluding the open *A* and downward fifth-position shift, bars 1 and 2 originate entirely from the same 10th-position *A* pentatonic major scale pattern we used in Ex. 30. The motif starting on beat *three* of bar 1 is a syncopated version of the hemiola from Examples 28 and 30. The lick arrives at the fifth-position *A* blues box for the flurry of 16th-note activity in bar 3 before landing on the IV-chord root on the downbeat of bar 4. Play Ex. 31 over bars 2–5 of the 12-bar "quick-change" progression.

Ex. 31

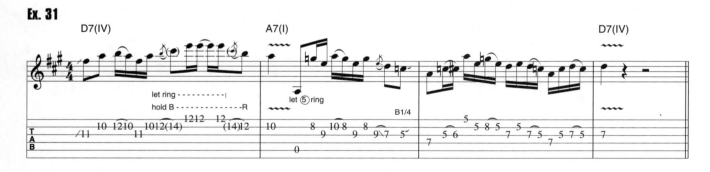

Example 32 — As you milk the 13th-position *A* pentatonic minor box over the IV chord (*D*) in the first two bars of Ex. 32, be sure to hold the opening half-note bend steady while you fret the adjacent high *G* with your 4th finger. It is possible to let both notes ring, but it's not required in this case. Next, re-attack the held bend, release it as notated, and shake the target *C* on beat *four*.

Bar 2 paraphrases the previous measure by altering its rhythms and adding a few more notes. This time the released bend is played as a grace note rather than over the space of two 16ths. As you return to the I chord in bar 3, you may recall the fifth-position phrase on beats *three* and *four* of bar 3 from Ex. 20. Try starting the lick using your neck pickup and switching to the bridge pickup at the halfway point.

The classic run in bar 4 is often employed as a turnaround, but here it is used to approach the V chord (*E*). Play Ex. 32 over bars 5–9 of the 12-bar progression.

Ex. 32

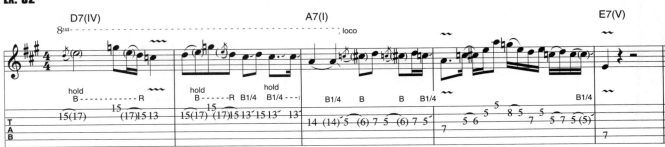

Example 33 explores three different rhythmic subdivisions of a double-stop–based motif over two bars of the I chord. Beat *one* features an oblique hammer-on followed by two repeats of the already hammered minor 3rd interval (*A* and *C*). On beat *two*, we morph into a syncopated 3/8 hemiola, which utilizes an oblique pull-off and is rhythmically displaced over beats *three* and *four*. (Try playing this five-note motif over the entire 12-bar progression.) In bar 2 we settle into a repetitive lick that is identical to the first four notes of the previous measure's hemiola. Play Ex. 33 over bars 1–2, 3–4, or bars 11–12 of the 12-bar progression.

Ex. 33

Example 34 — We'll wrap up this groove with the stratospheric IV–I–V lick in Ex. 34. Play the opening bendies and hammer/pull maneuver in the 17th-position *A* blues box (1st finger at the 17th fret), then slide into 14th position (1st finger at the 14th fret) for bar 2. We've seen similar pentatonic major licks, but this one treads the line between major and minor with a half-step bend to the ♭3 (*C*).

Shift back to 17th position and finish with the runs in bars 3, 4, and 5. Do you recall the fretboard shapes in bar 4? These adjacent bends and releases are a relative pentatonic minor adaptation of the second-position pentatonic major moves in Ex. 29 played an octave higher. Play Ex. 34 over bars 4–8 of the 12-bar progression.

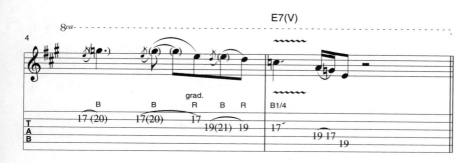

Groove #5
Moderate eighth- and 16th-note-based blues-rock.

Key: *A*   **Tempo:** ♩ = 102–128

Suggested accompaniment: A one-chord I-chord jam!

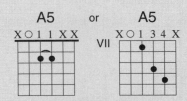

A5   or   A5
X O 1 1 X X   X O 1 3 4 X
VII

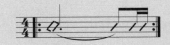

Tips: Once again, we'll be relying heavily on straight eighths, 16ths, and 16th-note triplets as we revisit and revamp many familiar moves. Though we're jamming over a single *A* chord, you'll discover that these examples have much in common with the ones from Groove #4. An interesting note: While Cream's extended jams were often framed by a single-chord accompaniment, they didn't necessarily rely on the I chord from the song's original key. Modulating to a new key for an extended solo section was one of the band's favorite compositional devices.

Recommended listening: Cream, "N.S.U" on *Live Cream, Vol. 1* (Universal).

Example 35 begins with some recognizable fifth-position *A* blues box riffing before sliding in and out of eighth position in bar 2. The 3/8 hemiola in bar 3 is broken into four notes and repeated four times over one-and-a-half measures. The lick morphs into four consecutive 16th-notes repeated on each beat for the remainder of the example.

Ex. 35

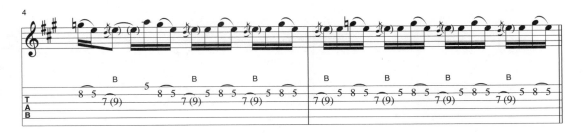

Example 36 — The first thing you should notice about bars 1 and 2 of Ex. 36 is their resemblance to bars 1 and 2 of Ex. 32. Though they use different rhythms and appear over different harmonic backgrounds, both have much in common.

In bar 3, finger an open *D7* chord shape on the top three strings, slide it into eighth position (1st finger at the 7th fret) to play the syncopated 16th-note dyads (let the 3rd string ring), and then slur down to the fifth-position *A* blues box for the hammered-and-pulled triplets on beat *three*. The repetitive 16th-note motif that takes shape in bar 4 is born on the last eighth-note in bar 3.

Ex. 36

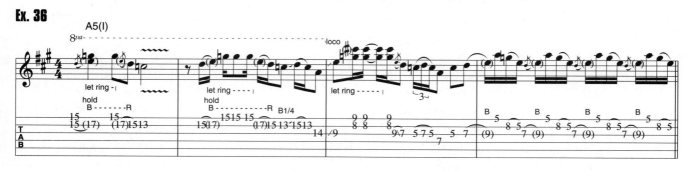

Groove #6 Slow 12/8 blues.

Key: C   **Tempo:** ♩ = 50–55

Suggested accompaniment: 12-bar slow-change blues progression with a I–IV–I–V turnaround (*C7–F7–C7–G7*) in bars 11 and 12. Comp on the illustrated I, IV, and V chords and their lower chromatic neighbors one half-step lower using this rhythm:

You can add eighth-note build-ups to the V-chord approach in bar 8 or the turnaround in bars 11 and 12. (Hint: Any chord may be approached from a half-step above or a half-step below.) For variety, try transposing the root–5 and root–6 voicings from Groove #2 to the key of *C* and applying the same rhythm here—played drastically slower, of course.

Tips: Though the denominator in 12/8 is an eighth-note, we count them in groups of three as dotted-quarter-note beats. Think of each beat as a mini-measure of 3/8 whose eighth-notes may be subdivided into 16th-notes, 16th-note triplets, 32nd-notes, etc. Each bar of 12/8 contains four of these 3/8 groupings.

Recommended listening: Cream, "Sleepy Time Time" on *Live Cream, Vol. 1.*

Example 37 consists of four distinct phrases. The half-step bend to the ♭5 (*G♭*) in bar 1 reveals that the first phrase is derived from the *C* blues scale.

You'll find a blend of *C* pentatonic major and *C* pentatonic minor at work in bar 2, while bar 3 covers all six strings in the eighth and sixth positions.

The fourth phrase is played in third position and features a knuckle-busting root–♭3 bend (*C–E♭*). These wide one-and-a-half-step bends and their rhythmic placement create tension and build momentum towards the IV chord (*F7*).

You can play Ex. 37 over bars 1–5 of the 12-bar quick-change progression, but it works equally well over bars 1–5 of the "slow-change" form.

Ex. 37

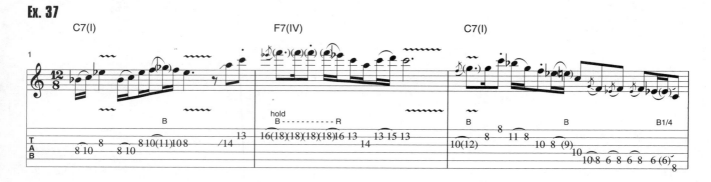

Groove #7

Moderately slow bluesy folk-rock ballad.

Key: D   **Tempo:** ♩ = 75–82

Suggested accompaniment: Travis-style fingerpicking for two beats on each chord shown except for the *D* in bar 4, which gets four beats. This forms a repetitive four-bar progression.

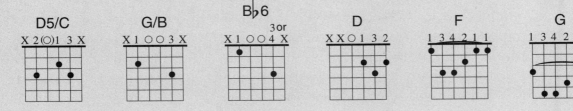

Travis-style hybrid fingerpicking

Tips: Somewhere between stints with Cream and Blind Faith, Clapton began incorporating a new tone—the 9— into his solos. This note soon became an important part of his blues-rock vocabulary, especially on Blind Faith's live electric versions of songs that had been recorded acoustically. In this case, we're adding *E* to the *D* pentatonic minor scale. If we blend this *E*, plus the 6 (*B*)—both of which are found in the *D* pentatonic major scale—with the *D* pentatonic minor scale, we get the *D* Dorian mode. Once again, the rhythmic emphasis throughout these examples is on straight eighths, 16ths, and 16th-note triplets.

Recommended listening: Blind Faith, "Can't Find My Way Home" on *Blind Faith* (Universal).

Example 38 mixes elements of all three previously discussed scales—*D* pentatonic minor, *D* pentatonic major, and *D* Dorian—within a single four-bar lick. We begin in the 10th-position *D* pentatonic minor blues box. (Remember this one from Groove #3?) While the call-and-response phrase in bars 1 and 2 is pure blues, the folky harmonic backdrop transforms it into something completely different. Both measures contain identical motifs, except we target a high *D* in bar 1 and drop it an octave in bar 2.

Bar 3 introduces the 9 (*E*) sandwiched between a slide from the ♭3 (*F*) one half-step higher and the root (*D*) a half-step lower. Of course, this description is in reference to the tonic key of *D*. Played against *F*—the chord of the moment—this three-note motif becomes a root–7–6 motif and gives off a temporary *Fmaj7/6* aroma. The *G* chord in the same measure is covered with a familiar *D* blues riff that slides from 10th to eighth position. In bar 4, the return to the *D* chord, we slip back to 10th position and inject a pair of 3's (*F#*'s) and a 6 (*B*) into the mix.

Ex. 38

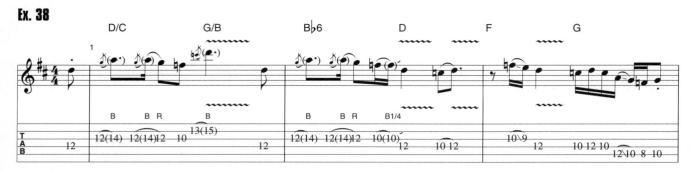

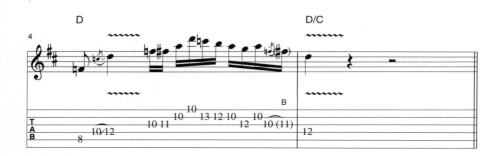

Example 39 — Like its predecessor, Ex. 39 begins somewhat sparsely in bars 1 and 2 before becoming busier in bars 3 and 4. The opening run spans two bars and makes use of the entire *D Dorian* mode. Note-wise it's little more than a descending scale—rhythm and phrasing are what gives this lick its air of elegance.

Play the first three notes with your 3rd finger, use your 1st finger for the slide from *F* to *E*, and grab the 12th fret with your 3rd finger. The ♭3–9 slide creates a momentary shift out of 10th position. In bar 2 you can shift to eighth position on beat *one* by playing the ♭7 (*C*) with your 3rd finger, or you may opt to play *C* and the *B–A* slide that follows using your 1st finger to shift positions on beat *two*. Either way, you land in eighth position.

Jump back to 10th position for bars 3 and 4's potent brew of pentatonicisms. The ♭3–9 slide makes a return appearance at the tail end of bar 4. Conduct your own harmonic analysis and discover how each part of the lick reacts to the chord of the moment.

Ex. 39

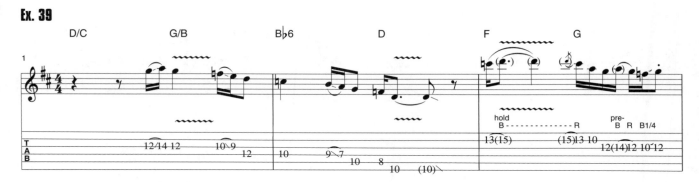

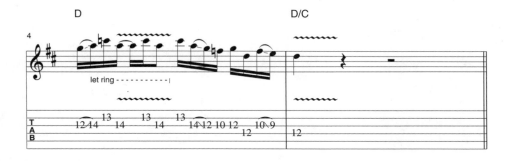

Example 40 shows a more urgent-sounding take on the same groove. Begin the 10th-position 3/8 hemiola on the second 16th note, or "ee," of beat *one* and repeat it seven times before breaking out of the pattern with a ♭7–4 move (*C* to *F*), a reverse *D* minor arpeggio, and a grace-note slide to eighth position in bar 2.

You've got barely a half-beat to make the leap to 13th position (3rd finger at the 15th fret) in bar 3, so be sure to have it in sight well ahead of time. The half-step bend to *A♭* brings the blues scale's ♭5 to the party. Release to *G*, pull off to *F*, and play the 4–root–♭3–9–root–v7–root lead-in back to 10th position.

The rhythmic syncopations in bar 4 contrast to the nearly steady stream of 16ths in the preceding measure. Though not a repetitive hemiola, the first three beats of this lick are phrased in 3/8, while beat *four* houses a fragment of the famous "Sunshine of Your Love" riff.

Ex. 40

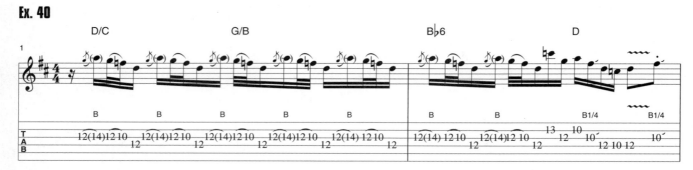

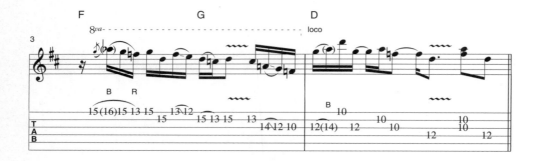

This concludes our visit to Claptonia. Learn these licks well and they'll be yours for life. Our next stop is Jeff Beckistan. Grab your passport and meet me at the border!

JEFF BECK

NEVER A BLUES PURIST, Jeff Beck cites Les Paul, Cliff Gallup, and the Tamla/Motown sound as early influences. Nevertheless, his style melds a heavily blues-oriented approach steeped in the sounds of Howlin' Wolf, Otis Rush, and Buddy Guy with a taste for the unpredictable and a sense of the absurd. Ranging from wildly raw to breathtakingly beautiful, Beck's playing can make you laugh and cry within a single heartbeat.

Beck's stint as Eric Clapton's successor in the Yardbirds fostered his experimental nature and resulted in numerous classic recordings, including one of the greatest guitar performances ever, "Jeff's Boogie" from *Over Under Sideways Down*. After leaving the Yardbirds in 1966, Beck flirted briefly with guitar instrumentals—including a recording of the pop ballad "Love Is Blue"—before putting together the first Jeff Beck Group. Kicking the power-trio format pioneered by Cream up a notch, Beck enlisted vocalist extraordinaire Rod Stewart as his front man and musical foil. The band, which also included Ron Wood on bass and the late Nicky Hopkins on piano, left two masterworks (*Truth* and *Beck-Ola*) and a string of spellbound audiences in its wake. Both albums are required listening.

An extended recovery period following a car crash put Beck out of commission until 1971, when he formed the second Jeff Beck Group. The quintet, featuring keyboardist Max Middleton and drummer Cozy Powell, emphasized a heavy update of the Motown sound, marking a radical stylistic departure for Beck—the first of many. With two more albums under his belt (*Rough and Ready* and *Jeff Beck Group*, also known as the "orange album"), Beck reverted to a power-trio lineup at the end of 1972, recruiting bassist Tim Bogert and drummer Carmine Appice for the collective known as BBA. His guest appearances on other artists' records also became more frequent.

Undoubtedly inspired by John McLaughlin's Mahavishnu Orchestra—particularly the group's synth pioneer and soon-to-be Beck bandmate Jan Hammer—1975's monumental *Blow by Blow* and its follow-up, *Wired* (which featured Hammer), found Beck veering head-on into the fusion arena, with spectacular results. These recordings, along with 1976's *Jeff Beck with the Jan Hammer Group Live*, struck a resonant chord with rock and jazz fans worldwide.

The wildest and most unpredictable of our triumvirate, Beck has also displayed the most stylistic growth. Beck has never been content to remain within a single genre for long; his post-'70s albums include a power-trio outing (*Guitar Shop*), a film score (*Frankie's House*), a tribute to rockabilly icon Gene Vincent and his legendary guitarist, Cliff Gallup (*Crazy Legs*), and three groundbreaking electronica-inspired outings (*Who Else!*, *You Had It Coming*, and *Jeff*)—reinventing himself nearly as many times along the way. (As the liner notes of my Japanese copy of *Jeff Beck—Session Works* so aptly put it: "He changes every minutes!")

Beck played a Fender Telecaster in the Yardbirds and favored the now-classic pairing of a Gibson Les Paul and a 100-watt Marshall stack for his first album as a leader. It wasn't long, however, before he began a slow conversion to the Fender Stratocaster. This transition took much longer than Clapton's seemingly overnight epiphany, as Beck straddled the line between Gibson and Fender for several years. By the latter part of the '70s, Beck became a full-fledged Strat-cat, eventually getting his own signature series Fender Stratocaster and abandoning his pick for an inimitable finger-and-whammy-bar style that continues to boggle the mind to this day. In addition to the Strat, you'll still catch him torturing a Tele on occasion.

Off-kilter bends, open-string and chromatic pulled-off triplets, unusual ornamentation, eastern Indian tonalities, and tongue-in-cheek humor are just a few of the parts you'll find in Beck's chop shop, where every note seems to be smeared with some kind of magical finger grease. Presented over seven different accompaniment grooves, the following Beck-style licks run the gamut from wild and crazy to, well, wilder and crazier. Buckle up and enjoy the ride!

JEFF BECK–Style Licks

Groove #1
Up-tempo shuffle with swing feel.

Key: G **Tempo:** ♩ = 192–208

Suggested accompaniment: Each 12-bar slow-change blues progression begins with a four-bar rhythm section breakdown. The only accompaniment here is a sharply accented I chord (G) on the downbeat of bar 1, plus improvised drum fills at the end of bar 4. The remainder of the progression melds the illustrated IV-, I-, and V-chord voicings (C9, G9, and D9) to an infectious shuffle-boogie rhythm. Shift each chord down a half-step on beat *two* and the "and" of beat *four*. These lower chromatic neighbors (B9, F#9, and C#9) create harmonic motion within each chord change and keep things swinging. Play C9–B9–C9–C9–B9–C9–B9–C9–C9 for the IV chord, G9–F#9– G9–G9–F#9– G9–F#9–G9–G9 for the I chord, and so on. Finish each lick with a C9 on the downbeat of the following measure.

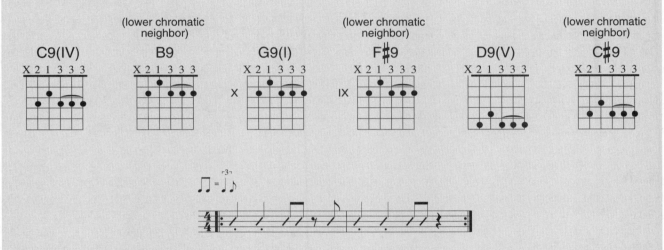

Tips: These four-bar snippets portray Beck's cheeky sense of humor and reveal some of his trickiest moves. They're designed to be played over the opening four-bar break and require no accompaniment.

Since they fly by pretty quickly, you get two licks per example. Like our first Clapton groove, a definite swing feel is present, but again the adjacent eighth-notes often breeze by as straight, not swung, eighths. Keep an eye out for the swung-eighth indicators in each example. When no indicator is shown, play even eighths. That said, there are plenty of flashy triplets and sleight-of-hand maneuvers present in these licks, and you'll be startled by the contrast between Beck's and Clapton's rhythmic and melodic approaches to similar harmonic terrain.

Recommended listening: The Yardbirds, "Jeff's Boogie" on *Over Under Sideways Down/Roger the Engineer* (Repertoire) and other Yardbirds collections.

Examples 41a and 41b — sly takes on "Mary Had a Little Lamb"—reflect Beck's penchant for off-the-cuff (and often out-of-context) quotations. The simple singsong melody is dressed up in 6th harmonies and swung heavily. Use hybrid picking (pick and middle finger) to claw both notes simultaneously, and apply palm muting as indicated.

The first two bars of each example are essentially the same, while bars 3 and 4 differ considerably. Example 41a features chromatically descending major 6ths embellished with slippery slides and signature "zips" up the high-*E* and down the low-*E* strings. (The last three notes sound cool as written, but don't worry about hitting these specific pitches in the heat of battle; just nail the rhythm with plenty of attitude.) In Ex. 41b, each descending major-6th shape is transformed into a partial dominant-7 chord by inserting an additional note one whole-step lower on the *G* string. Arpeggiate the chord shapes and let them ring as shown, or cut each note short for a staccato variation.

Ex. 41a

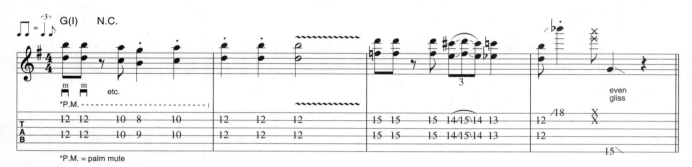

Ex. 41b

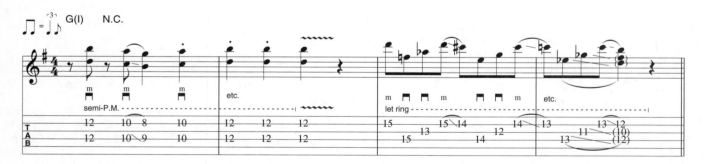

Examples 42a and 42b — another set of humorous paraphrases—utilize natural harmonics to simulate Big Ben's chimes. With unmistakable style and attitude, Example 42a combines the entire Big Ben melody—played as quarter-notes—and the theme from *Alfie*, a classic '60s flick. Example 42b quotes Ben's first four notes for two beats apiece. The two-bar response comes in the form of a quartet of repetitive triplet pull-offs, a *G* half-note target, and a ride down the low-*E* string. The inclusion of *C#*—the #4 of *G*—is a cool touch that throws these triplets noticeably off kilter.

Ex. 42a

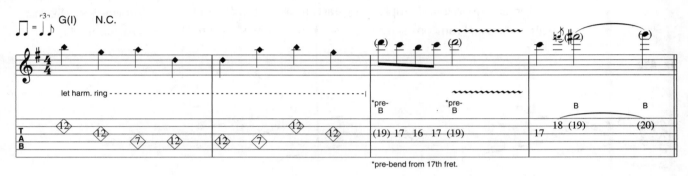

*pre-bend from 17th fret.

Ex. 42b

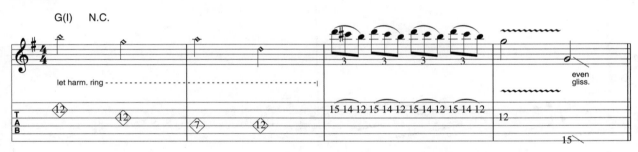

Examples 43a and 43b illustrate more Beck-style eighth-note triplet pull-offs. Example 43a begins with two bars of identically shaped sixth-fret/third-fret/open-string pull-offs alternating between the 1st and 2nd strings. In bars 3 and 4, we shift to the 3rd and 4th strings and reduce the fret-span of each triplet by a half-step. Notice how the fretted portions of these triplets outline a third-position *G* pentatonic minor scale pattern. Try this lick with or without palm muting.

For Ex. 43b, wait until beat *two* to begin alternating symmetrical two-whole-step shapes between the *B* and *E* strings, then shift to a whole-step/half-step configuration on beat *two* of bar 2. In bar 3, we half-time the eighth-note triplet rhythm and play each previous whole-step/half-step shape as a descending quarter-note triplet with staccato phrasing. Bar 4 maintains the quarter-note triplet feel with an unusual run consisting of a ♭3–3 bend followed by a root–♭7–5–♭5–♭3 motif.

Ex. 43a

Ex. 43b

Examples 44a and 44b combines selected eighth-note triplets from Ex. 43a and 43b to form a call-and-response lick played in contrasting upper and middle registers. Milk the penultimate ♭3–3 (B♭–B) bend gradually and give the target root a good shake.

Characterized by chromatic ascending triplet pull-offs, Ex. 44b is a textbook exercise in creating tension through sheer momentum. As you play each triplet you'll want to look ahead to line up the next 4th-finger/fret position. Try this move on any string, or alternate between any pair of adjacent strings.

Ex. 44a

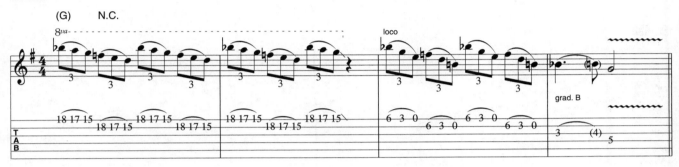

Ex. 44b

Examples 45a and 45b — The pulled-off eighth-note triplets in Ex. 45a pay homage to Les Paul and Cliff Gallup, two of Beck's chief influences. This symmetrical half-step/whole-step shape traverses the top four strings, leaving many non-chord and non-scale tones in its wake—another example of sheer melodic momentum.

Remember all of those three-against-four hemiola rhythms in the previous Clapton-style licks? Beck's take on the same concept might look and sound something like the chromatically ascending straight eighths in the first half of Ex. 45b. The "answer" phrase in bars 3 and 4 is a simple but effective series of descending chromatic eighth-note triplets, each consisting of a hammered-and-pulled whole-step.

Ex. 45a

Ex. 45b

Examples 46a and 46b — Hybrid pick-and-middle-finger picking makes a return appearance for the tension-laden ascending chromatic octaves in Ex. 46a. After the initial low *G* is played, a three-note pattern emerges; the upper octave is clawed with the middle finger and then followed by two picked downstrokes on the lower octave. Each subsequent three-note grouping ascends one half-step. This forms a rhythmically displaced 3/8 hemiola that starts on the "and" of beat *one*.

Try adding a touch of palm muting, or, if you want to play it Beck-style 2000, lose the pick and go at it with your thumb and index finger. You can up the ante on this already tense lick by adding a constant, exaggerated vibrato, as shown.

Example 46b combines two techniques: A pair of eighth-note triplet pull-offs provides the call, while the response features more hybrid-picked ascending octaves, played this time on the *A* and *G* strings. By starting on *D* and ending on *F#*, we create the illusion of a momentary V chord (*D*). Experiment with different degrees of palm muting, or skip it and add vibrato instead.

Ex. 46a

Ex. 46b

Examples 47a and 47b — Sporting the sickest moves of the lot, Examples 47a and 47b provide two takes on the same skewed banjo lick. Example 47a features what at first appears to be four curious and unrelated chord shapes, but closer inspection of these clusters reveals the addition of a note one half-step below the lowest G chord tone in each one. If you had to label them, you could call them *Gsus#4*, *G6♭9* (or *Esus#4*), *Gmaj7* (or *Emadd9*), and *Gsus#4*. The rhythmic pattern is a simple blend of quarter- and half-notes. Finger each chord shape and use hybrid picking (pick, middle, and ring fingers) to sound all three notes simultaneously. Keep the quarter-notes in bars 1 and 2 short, as indicated, but give them full rhythmic value in bar 3. Wrap it up with a low-G root and trademark slide down the low-E string in bar 4.

In Ex. 47b, we play each chord shape from Ex. 47a as an ascending three-note arpeggio. Let each one ring before you cross strings to the next. Essentially a banjo roll, this technique works best sans pick. (If you must, give pick–middle–ring a try.) The final zip up and down the low-E string serves as an instrumental "woo!"

You can also whip yourself into a frenzy by playing the first three notes in bar 1 or 3 as an eighth-note triplet and moving the figure up the neck chromatically. Try playing single or twin triplets at each fret position—just don't hurt yourself!

Ex. 47a

Ex. 47b

Examples 48a and 48b — Example 48a also plays musical Q-and-A: An ascending *G* pentatonic minor sequence in bars 1 and 2 poses the question, while the flurry of eighth-note triplet pull-offs in bars 3 and 4 provide the answer. This time, the pulled-off triplets cover all six strings and outline the entire third-position *G* pentatonic minor box pattern.

Beck often used his "Boogie" breaks to pay homage to his peers, and Ex. 48b, our final Groove #1 lick, acknowledges a friendly rivalry between Yardbirds alumni with a sassy paraphrasing of Clapton's then tour-de-force "Stepping Out." (See Clapton Groove #1.)

Ex. 48a

Ex. 48b

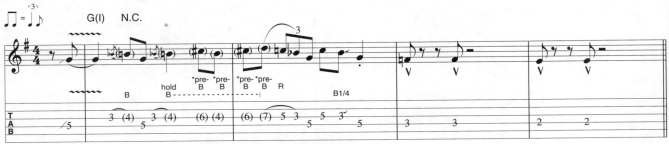

*pre-bend *C#* from 5th fret and *B* from 3rd fret.

Groove #2

Moderately slow, heavy blues-rock shuffle.

Key: B   **Tempo:** ♩ = 96–106

Suggested accompaniment: A 12-bar slow-change blues progression featuring a single-note I-chord riff (root–root–octave–♭7–octave–♭7-5, or *B–B–B–A–B–A–F#*; see grids) transposed to the IV and V chords based on the following swing-eighth rhythm figure.

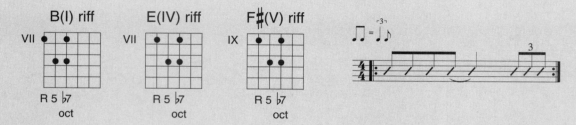

B(I) riff   **E(IV) riff**   **F#(V) riff**

R 5 ♭7 oct   R 5 ♭7 oct   R 5 ♭7 oct

Tips: For an accompaniment variation, replace the last three notes in every other measure with the 4, #4, and 5 of each chord (*E–E#–F* for the I chord, etc.). For maximum authenticity, have your bassist play the same notes with the following rhythm throughout the progression. The guitar and bass parts combine to create a cool, loping push/pull groove.

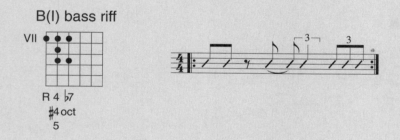

B(I) bass riff

R 4 ♭7
#4 oct
5

Recommended listening: Jeff Beck Group (I), "Rock My Plimsoul" on *Truth* (Epic).

Example 49 — You'll find that the slower shuffle rhythm that frames the following licks accommodates much more rhythmic complexity than our previous groove. Beck has always had a flair for combining straight-16th-note rhythms with swung eighths and eighth-note triplets, and the 10th-position pickup to Ex. 49 provides a perfect illustration. Many players would simply round the first note off to the second eighth-note in an eighth-note triplet, but phrasing it slightly sooner on the second 16th-note of beat *three* imparts a jagged and more urgent rhythmic feel that is an important component of the Beck sound.

After you nail the pickup, slide a pair of swung eighths from *A* to *G#* for a signature Beck move that floats a sus4–3 suspension and resolution over the IV chord (*E7*). Add an extra note for the all-

16th-based pickup into bar 2, and skip the suspension in bar 3 by heading directly for the *G♯*. For the return to the I chord (*B7*) in bar 4, we rapidly trill between *B* pentatonic minor scale tones (6–root, 5–♭7, and ♭3–4) before dropping into seventh position to target *D♯*, the 3 of the tonic *B*. Slide between the first two trills, and then jump to the *G* string to nail the third. Play Ex. 49 over bars 5 through 8 of the 12-bar blues progression.

Ex. 49

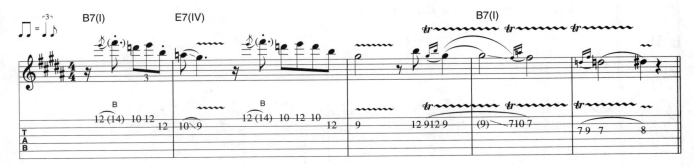

Example 50 — Expanding the idea from our previous lick, Ex. 50 spans all six strings with rapid trills to cover the IV–I change. The pickup and bar 1 are derived entirely from the seventh-position *B* pentatonic minor box, while bar 2 drops in and out of fifth position. Returning to the I chord in bar 3, we flutter between the ♭7 and root before venturing outside *B* pentatonic minor territory with ♭3–3 and 5–6 trills on beats *two* and *three*. Complete the lick with the B.B. King special in bar 4, customized here to Beck specs by substituting a 3 (*D♯*) for the more common ♭3 (*D*). Play Ex. 50 over bars 5 through 8 of the 12-bar blues progression.

Ex. 50

Example 51 — In Ex. 51, we employ the *B* pentatonic major scale plus the ♭3 and 4 in a four-bar call-and-response lick played over the I chord. Begin by using your 2nd finger to slide from the ♭3 to the 3 (*G* to *G#*). This aligns your 1st finger in 12th position, where you'll remain for the entire lick except for a brief 1st-finger dip to the 11th fret at the end of bar 1. The response features an identical pickup into bar 3 followed by a sustained 2–3 (*C#–D#*) bend and subsequent laid-back 16th-note release. Bend with your 3rd finger and grab the 14th-fret *F#* with your 4th finger. The delayed phrasing on the 16ths in bar 3 and the rhythmic bend in bar 4 are two more Beck hallmarks. Play Ex. 51 over bars 1 through 4 of the 12-bar blues progression.

Ex. 51

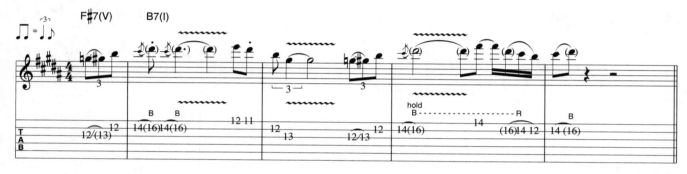

Example 52 portrays the return to the I chord via the IV (*E7–B7*) and may be dropped into bars 7 and 8 of the 12-bar progression. Align your fret hand in 12th position, play the syncopated partial triplet in the pickup, and then reinforce your grip and go for the ultra-wide root–3 (*B–D#*) bend on the downbeat of bar 1. Dance between the root and ♭7 on beats *two* and *three*, repeat the chromatic ♭3–3–4 climb for three beats, trill the ♭3–3, and finish with a root–5–root triplet.

Ex. 52

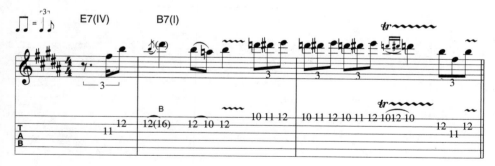

Example 53 — The two-bar turnaround in Ex. 53 reprises some of the flash from our Groove #1 licks and offers an interesting reverse hemiola technique—four-against-six, or two-against-three, versus the usual three-against-two rhythmic displacement. Be sure to observe the difference in phrasing between sextuplets, which tend to be grouped in "twos," and twin 16th-note triplets, which are grouped in "threes." Play Ex. 53 over bars 11 and 12 of the 12-bar progression.

Ex. 53

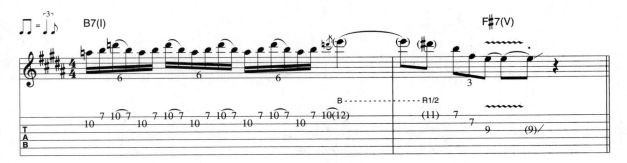

Example 54 illustrates Beck's penchant for hybrid-picked trills between notes on adjacent strings. Playing steady sextuplets, we alternate sustained bends on the 2nd string with a 1st-string pedal tone to suggest partial I, IV, and V chords. Anchor your 4th finger on *F#* (1st string/14th fret) and your 3rd finger on *C#* (2nd string/14th fret), and begin with a half-step bend to *D*. This covers the pickup measure and two bars of *E7* with an *F#–D* trill that locks in perfectly with the IV chord because *D* and *F#* are the ♭7 and 9 of *E7*. Without releasing the previous bend, prebend the *B* string an additional half-step to *D#* to cover the I chord in bars 3 and 4. This gives us the *D#* and *F#*—the 3 and 5 of *B7*. Prebend another half-step—for a total of one-and-a-half steps—to play the *F#–E* trill over the V chord (*F#7*) in bar 5. Drop the bend a whole-step for the IV change in bar 6, then prebend another half-step to cover the return to the I chord in bar 7. Hint: Concentrate on nailing those high *F#*s as steady eighth-note triplets with your middle finger, and the picked offbeat bends will fall into place more naturally. Play Ex. 54 over bars 4 through 11 of the 12-bar progression.

Ex. 54

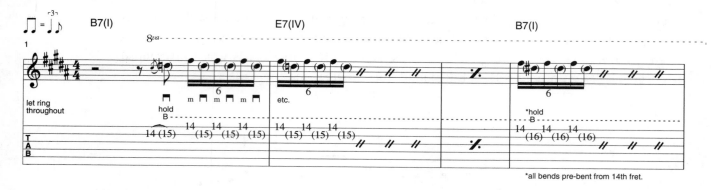

*all bends pre-bent from 14th fret.

Example 55 — Beck's improvised trade-offs with vocalist Rod Stewart are legendary—and something Jimmy Page would fancy enough to bring to his post-Yardbirds band, Led Zeppelin. Example 55 covers the I–IV–I change with four distinctly different variations of the same melody. The measure of rest that follows each one-bar lick is left open for a vocal response. In bar 1, we alternate a held bend to the 5 (F#) with a ♭7 (A). Bar 3 paraphrases the same motif by changing the last note and delaying it by half a beat. And while Beck plays wicked slide guitar, the IV-chord and I-chord licks in bars 5 and 7 show how far back he started emulating this sound sans slide. Try transposing all of these licks to the next set of adjacent higher strings. Play Ex. 55 over bars 1 through 8 of the 12-bar progression.

Ex. 55

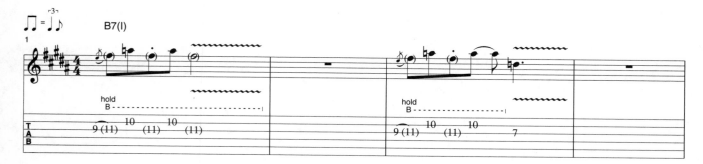

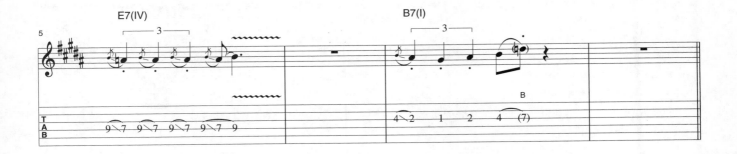

Example 56 follows suit with another eight-bar round of trade-offs; however, the vocal calls now precede the guitar responses. A muted string rake leads into the opening melodic bend in bar 2, and once again eighth-note triplets, swung eighths, and even 16ths mingle within the same measure.

This example also marks our first glimpse of Beck's unique brand of microtonal bendies, notated throughout as quarter-step bends. The little even-eighth snippet on beat *four* of bar 2 is an important part of Beck's musical vocabulary that shouldn't be taken lightly. Don't worry about bending exactly one quarter-step—just use your ear to place the bend somewhere between the ♭3 (*D*) and 3 (*D♯*), and practice this move until it moans. Hint: Try pre-microbending the pulled-off *D* note as you pull off to it. The goal is to make it sound as sick as possible—in a good way!

The unreleased prebend in bar 4 is another secret weapon in Beck's massive arsenal of phrasing techniques. More *faux* slide sounds—this time utilizing grace-note releases from prebends as opposed to actual finger slides—surface in the IV-chord lick in bar 6. In bar 8 we wrap up this groove with a simple but effective move that incorporates a reverse grace-note slide, two microtonal bends, a hammer-on, and vibrato in just four beats. Bloody marvelous! Play Ex. 56 over bars 1 through 8 of the 12-bar progression.

Ex. 56

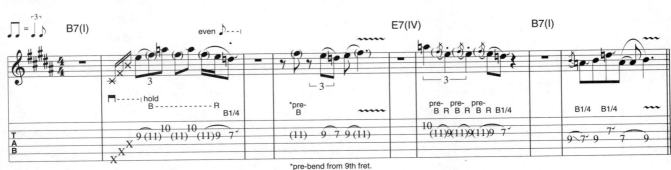

*pre-bend from 9th fret.

Groove #3   Funky 16th-note blues/rock.   Key: *F#*   Tempo: ♩ = 82–96

Suggested accompaniment: Another 12-bar slow-change blues progression, this one utilizes a funky 16th-note feel laced with Motown-influenced bass figures improvised over the I, IV, and V chords (*F#7, B9,* and *C#9*). For example, try combining a root–octave–5–octave–3–4–#4–5 I-chord riff (*F#–F#–C#–F#–A#–B–B#–C#*) with the following rhythm.

F#7(I) bass riff

R 3 oct
4
#4
5

You can also comp similar syncopated rhythms using these I-, IV-, and V-chord voicings:

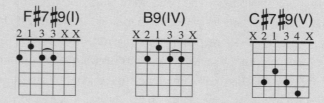

F#7#9(I)   B9(IV)   C#7#9(V)

Tips: The key of *F#* may be an uncommon choice for many rockers, but it has a nasty, clangorous quality that serves Beck well. The slower tempo also accommodates Beck's penchant for 16th-note triplets and funky, syncopated rhythms.

Recommended listening: Jeff Beck Group (I), "Let Me Love You" on *Truth* (Epic).

Examples 57a and 57b — Shifting gears to a funky 16th blues-rock groove, Examples 57a and 57b show a pair of variations on the same concept—a sheet of sound that blankets the I chord (*F#7*) with the entire second-position *F#* blues box and plenty of 16th-note action. You'll find several similarities in bar 1 of each example, but their second measures feature considerably different approaches: In bar 2 of Ex. 57a we shift to funky syncopated octaves played with hybrid picking and palm muting on the 6th string, while Ex. 57b follows through with a growling 16th-note continuation of bar 1. Make 'em sound as nasty as possible. Play Examples 57a and 57b over bars 1–2, 3–4, or 7–8 in the 12-bar progression.

Ex. 57a

Ex. 57b

Example 58 — A short ascending chromatic run precedes the ♭7 of both the V (*C#7#9*) and IV (*B9*) chords during the four-bar turnaround lick in Ex. 58. (There's a root-♭7 variation on beat *one* of bar 1.) Bars 3 and 4 house another children's song quote; this time, it's "Shortnin' Bread," played first in the low register and then repeated one octave higher. Try reversing the order of the last two measures for a high-to-low variation. Play Ex. 58 over bars 9 through 12 of the 12-bar progression.

Ex. 58

Example 59 — Still another four-bar turnaround, Ex. 59 features hybrid-picked ascending chromatic octaves over the V and IV chords (*C#7#9* and *B9*). Think you've heard it before? Not quite. These broken octaves ascend chromatically from the root to the 3 of each chord, but the twist is to play them using a syncopated 3/8 hemiola grouped as alternating pairs of 16th- and eighth-notes for three beats. Both bars 1 and 2 end with an additional 16th-note on beat *four*, followed by the 3 of each chord played as an unbroken octave. Apply palm muting at your own discretion.

The drop to a second-position I-chord riff in bars 3 and 4 is a proto-metal device that Beck practically invented. The ♭7–3 double-stops played on beat *two* of each measure emit a bad-ass *F#7#9* tonality, and the ascending chromatic double-stops in bar 3—"dragged" as an eighth-note triplet—kick the bad-boy factor up another notch. Play Ex. 59 over bars 9 through 12 of the 12-bar progression.

Ex. 59

Example 60 — Like the first example in our previous groove (see Ex. 49), the IV–I lick in Ex. 60 commences on the second 16th of beat *one*. The bulk of bar 1—played in fourth position—sets up the approach to *D#*, the 3 of *B9*, with a suspension and resolution (also similar to Ex. 49) in bar 2. After dancing around this key chord tone, we move back to the I for a less ornamented but equally cool line that utilizes a one-and-a-half-step bend and delayed release before dropping us into second position. Milk that quarter-step bend in bar 4 until it moos for mercy! Play Ex. 60 over bars 5 through 8 of the 12-bar progression.

Ex. 60

Examples 61a and 61b — Here's a bonus two-fer: Examples 61a and 61b are frisky 14th-position *F#* blues box romps that are a joy to play. You've probably heard and played the opening two-beat motif in Ex. 61a many times before, but Beck manages to make it his own with a combination of smooth and choppy phrasing and mojo magic. (Actually, the same goes for most of these licks.) The ♭3–3–5–root–♭7–root–♭7 run (*A–A#–C#–F#–E–F#–E*) that follows on beats *three* and *four* almost seems to mock the opening motif (minus the bend). While these aren't staccato 16ths, you'll want to chop them off slightly for a more authentic Beck vibe. Take a mental snapshot of the 32nd- and 16th-note motif on beat *one* of bar 2—you'll be seeing it again in the near future. We finish up with a descending ♭3–root–5 move (*A–F#–C#*), tag on the 6 (*D#*), and then bend and release the *D* string from the root to the ♭3 and back again.

In Ex. 61b we move the opening motif from the previous example back one beat and commence with a 2nd-finger slide into 14th position (2nd finger at the 15th fret), followed by an oblique unison bend—shaken, not stirred. Remember that lick from the beginning of bar 2 in the previous example? Well, here it is again, played on beat *two* with the 32nd-note pull-off shifted over to the second 16th. Subtle and cool—that's how to play this game. Utilizing a different three-note pickup, bar 2 appears to be identical to bar 1 sans the unison bend, but look closely at the motif on beat *two*; the last two notes have been changed to *A#* and *F#* and now reflect an *F#7* arpeggio. The final move is a bend to the 4 (*B*) and half-step release to the 3 (*A#*). That is some shweet shtuff. Of course, you'll want to transpose both licks down an octave to second position. Play Examples 61a and 61b over bars 1 and 2 of the 12-bar progression.

Ex. 61a

Ex. 61b

Example 62 — At first, the IV-chord lick in Ex. 62 may appear to be a simple 3/8 hemiola, but there's more to the big picture. Check it out: The first three notes (*E–C#–A*) establish the basic three-against-four pattern with a sophisticated 11–9–♭7 motif. When this is repeated, we add a 32nd-note-triplet pull-off to the second 16th beat, then repeat the new figure twice. This brings us to beat *four*, where we start the whole deal over again for the next three beats. Halfway through bar 2, we break out of the hemiola with a jump to the 19th fret for an anticipated whole-step bend to the ♭3 and return to the root. Play Ex. 62 over bars 5 and 6 of the 12-bar progression.

Ex. 62

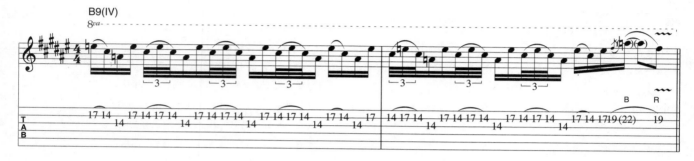

Example 63 — Dropping back to the second-position *F#* blues scale—that's *F#* pentatonic minor plus *C*, the ♭5—begin the flurry of 16th-note activity in Ex. 63 with either your 4th finger or 3rd finger. Short, sweet, and to the point, this lick covers all six strings and brings this groove to its conclusion. Play Ex. 63 over bars 1–2, 3–4, or 7–8 of the 12-bar progression.

Ex. 63

Groove #4

Slow 12/8 blues
with straight eighth–note feel.

Key: *G*   **Tempo**: ♩ = 40–44

Suggested accompaniment: Twelve-bar slow–change blues progression with an I–IV–I–V turnaround (*G7–C9–G7–D9*) in bars 11 and 12. Comp on the illustrated I, IV, and V chords and their chromatic neighbors one half-step lower using a rhythm figure similar to the one in Clapton Groove #6. You can add eighth-note build-ups to the V-chord approach in bar 8 or the turnaround in bars 11 and 12. (Reminder: Any chord may be approached from a half-step above or a half-step below.)

G9(I)

C9(IV)

D9(V)

Tips: Partition each measure into four 3/8 groupings and practice each dotted-quarter beat as its own 3/8 entity, and you'll find that these rhythms aren't as complex as they look. For further clarity, you can double the value of each note and count each dotted-quarter beat as a measure of 3/4. Incidentally, this kind of partitioning and note-value doubling is applicable to any time signature.

Recommended listening: Jeff Beck Group (I), "Blues Deluxe" and "You Shook Me" on *Truth* (Epic), and "Sweet Little Angel" and "The Sun Is Shining"–if you can find live recordings.

Example 64 — Beck didn't record many slow blues standards, but they were plentiful in his first group's live repertoire. As mentioned previously, slow 12/8 blues licks can look like a nightmare on paper. Slow tempos allow you to cram more events into each beat simply because there is more time available to do so. Let's use the one-bar, IV-chord (C9) line in Ex. 64 to illustrate how to make these licks easier to read.

When we double the note values, the pickup becomes an eighth-note triplet played quarter-eighth, or as swung eighths. The events on beat *one* are transformed into a quarter-note tied to the first note of an eighth-note triplet followed by a pair of straight eighth-notes. Get the idea? Beat *two* becomes four 16th-notes, plus the first two notes of an eighth-note triplet followed by two 16ths and an eighth-note. Practice each beat very slowly until its rhythm becomes ingrained, and then string them together and gradually increase the tempo. In addition to the crammed phrasing, check out the final move at the end of beat *two*—a half-step bend/release pulled off to a microtonal prebend. Hmm, sound familiar? Play Ex. 64 over bars 4, 5, or 10 of the 12-bar slow-change progression. This one also works just as well over the I (*G7*) and V (*D9*) chords.

Ex. 64

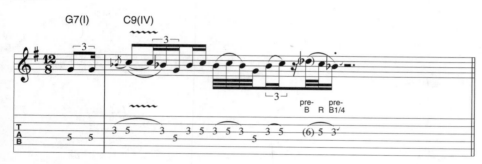

Example 65 begins with signature Beck-style swagger as descending oblique unisons laced with heavy vibrato outline the IV chord's 4, 3, 2, root, and ♭7 (*F, E, D, C,* and *B♭*), and lead us to the hesitant stop-and-start bursts in bar 2. On beat *four*, the lick picks up momentum, morphing into a blindingly fast 32nd-note-triplet extravaganza that lasts for two full beats—six triplet pull-offs per dotted-quarter beat. The short lick on beat *three* is an elongated version of the one that ends Ex. 64. Play Ex. 65 over bars 6 and 7 of the 12-bar slow-change progression.

Ex. 65

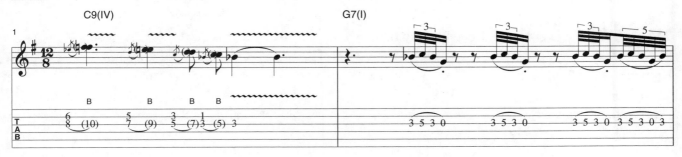

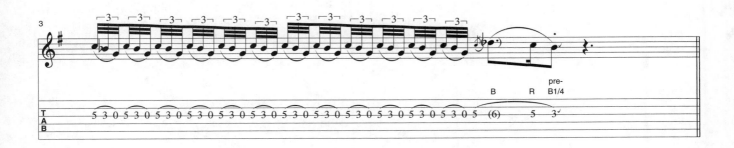

Example 66 — Our final slow blues lick is rhythmically simplistic by comparison. Example 66 consists of an unbroken chain of 16th-note triplets spanning beats *one* and *two* and all but the last 16th of beat *three*. Begin in 15th position and use your 3rd finger to shuttle between the ♭7s (*F*'s) and Beck-approved prebent *G* roots before starting beat *two*'s journey across the bottom four strings. Shift to 13th position by grabbing the *G* on the downbeat of dotted-quarter beat *three* with your 2nd finger and the following *B♭* with your 1st finger. Play Ex. 66 over bar 1, 2, 3, 4, 7, 8, 11, or 12 of the 12-bar slow-change progression. This lick works equally well over the IV (*C9*) and V (*D9*) chords.

Ex. 66

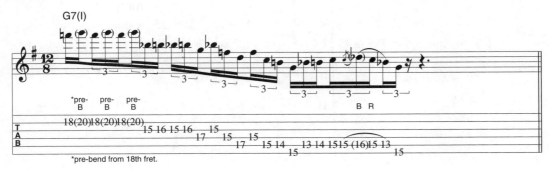

Groove #5

Chugging 16th-note blues-rock.

Key: G **Tempo:** ♩ = 80–90

Suggested accompaniment: *A* 12-bar slow-change blues progression powered by 16th-note I, IV, and V chords (*G5, C5,* and *D7#9*), and a heavy, single-note I-chord riff (root–♭7–4–♭3–root, or *G–F–C–B♭–G*) played as contrasting quarter-notes in bars 2, 6, and 10. You can also play this riff using the illustrated root–5 power chords.

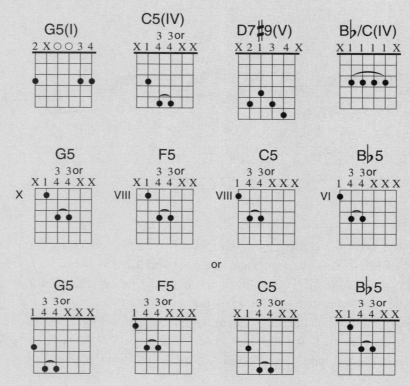

Tips: You don't have to pump 16ths for every chorus. Try playing the I, IV, and V changes in bars 1, 5, and 9 as whole-note power chords and substituting the illustrated B♭/C chord for the IV (*C5*). This sounds great when you play the main I-chord riff in bars 2, 6, and 10 using 16th-note power chords.

Recommended listening: Jeff Beck Group, "Going Down" on *Jeff Beck Group* (II) (Epic) and various Beck collections.

Example 67 — Situated at the top end of the 15th-position *G* blues box, the two-bar I-chord lick in Ex. 67 shows how to get supreme melodic mileage out of just three fretted notes. Follow the opening no-nonsense bend and root–♭7–5–v7 run (*G–F–D–F*) with a syncopated jig between the ♭7 and root, and then inject the slick hammer-on/pull-off move on beat *two* of bar 2. Like most Beck-style licks, *when* you play is as important as *what* you play. The final bend is held and vibrated twice as long as the opening one; it's a cool touch that ties the whole thing together. Play Ex. 67 over bars 1–2, 3–4, 7–8, or 11–12 of the 12-bar slow-change progression. This lick works equally over the IV chord (*C9*).

Ex. 67

Example 68 — At this tempo, the pulled-off 16th-note triplets in Ex. 68 are nearly identical to the eighth-note triplets scattered throughout Groove #1. Begin in 12th position, use your 4th finger to fret the high *G*, then pull off to the 12th fret and open-*E* notes—you know the routine. Moving this familiar shape to the 12th position creates a root–6–6 motif over the I chord. Play this triplet three times, and then alternate it with the same shape on the *B* string for the remainder of the measure. You'll recognize the first two beats in bar 2—third-position pull-offs that outline a descending *G* pentatonic minor scale—from our first Beck groove. The barless dive-bomb on beats *three* and *four* is a technique pioneered by Beck in the late '60s and early '70s. This time, accuracy definitely counts. Practice sliding into whole-step grace-note bends to build accuracy before stretching them the extra whole-step. Play Ex. 68 over bars 1–2, 3–4, 7–8, or 11–12 of the 12-bar slow-change progression.

Ex. 68

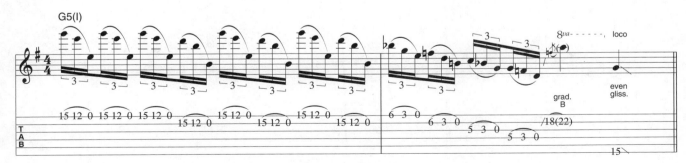

Example 69 — The 3/16 hemiola in Ex. 69—subdivided into a 16th–32nd–32nd–16th grouping—incorporates a double pull-off between its last three notes. You could sound all four notes with a single attack, but this is less controllable and changes the character of the lick. This root–♭3–root–6 motif (*G–B♭–G–E*) functions as 5–♭7–5–3 of the IV chord, essentially transforming it into a *C7* arpeggio. Play the motif ten times, and then anticipate the bent *G* on the return to the I chord. The prebent *B* in bar 3 is played as a silent half-step release from the previous whole-step bend. Try following this one with an elongated bar-long version of the barless dive-bomb from the previous example. Play Ex. 69 over bars 5 through 7 of the 12-bar slow-change progression.

Ex. 69

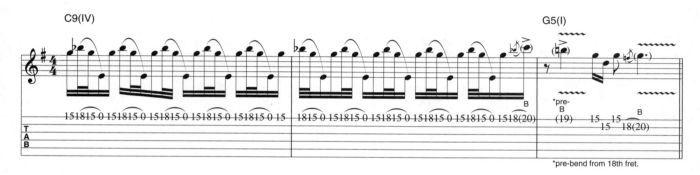

Example 70 — The four-bar turnaround shown in Ex. 70 begins with a sneaky V-chord move. Following the two-note pickup, we play a rhythmic bend from *F* to *F#*, but the bend actually originates from *E* at the 17th fret. The trick is to prebend the *E* one half-step to *F* on beat *one*, and bend another half-step to *F#* a 16th-note later. Once there, hold the bend while you play the high *A* on beat *two*, and then pick and release the bend back to the 17th-fret *E*. Follow up with a pair of syncopated *D*'s and you've nailed the first phrase.

The IV-chord (*C9*) lick in bar 2 brims with rhythmic syncopations that revolve around squirmy, microtonal *C*'s and contrasting whole- and half-step grace-note hammer-ons. In bars 3 and 4 we tread the thin line between major and minor tonalities before finally conceding to a bent 3 (*B*) and wrapping up Groove #5. Play Ex. 70 over bars 9 through 12 of the 12-bar slow-change progression.

Ex. 70

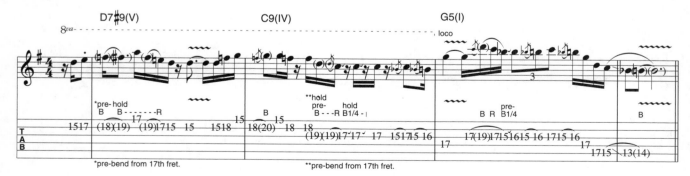

Groove #6

Medium-tempo reggae-rock with half-time feel.

Key: *A*   **Tempo**: ♩ = 75–82

Suggested accompaniment: A repetitive, one-bar I–IV vamp (*A–D*). Play each chord for two beats using either of the following rhythms:

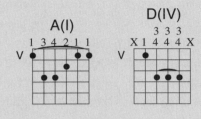

Tips: When a lick utilizes a swung–16th feel, try swinging the 16th-notes in the accompaniment, like this:

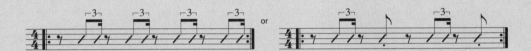

Recommended listening: Jeff Beck with the Jan Hammer Group, "She's a Woman" on *Jeff Beck with the Jan Hammer Group Live* (Epic).

Example 71 — Played fingerstyle in the fifth position, Ex. 71 combines eighth- and 16th-notes plus their triplet counterparts with both *A* pentatonic major and minor elements in a funky, blues-tinged reggae outing. After the opening slide into the 3 (*C#*) and syncopated root–♭7 (*A–G*), we begin a string of bluesy eighth-note triplets that span the remainder of bar 1 plus the first beat of bar 2. We're zeroing in on some key chord tones, so you can really hear the chord changes within the lick itself. Notice how *C#*—the 3 of *A*—is the targeted downbeat in three out of four measures.

Bar 3 contains two prebend/release/pull-off maneuvers. The first—a 16th-note triplet on beat *one*—features a half-step bend, while the second utilizes a whole-step on the last three 16ths of beat *three*. The subtle whammy-bar work in bar 4 is laced with typically unpredictable rhythms and hints at the unprecedented control of the device Beck has since developed. (Since we're only tracing Beck's stylistic path through 1975, his extraordinary whammy style will have to wait for Volume 2.) Pull off to *C#* from *D* in the previous measure and gradually depress the bar very slightly to lower the note a half-step to *C* by the last 16th of beat *one*. With the bar still depressed, play the 4th string at the 7th fret to sound the *G* grace-note, and then immediately release the bar to sound the *A* half-note on beat *two*. (Note: Due to the difference in string gauges, the bar bends will lower the *G* and *D* strings different degrees.) Pull off to *G* on beat *four* and drop the bar another half-step to sound *F#* on the following upbeat and you're home free.

Ex. 71

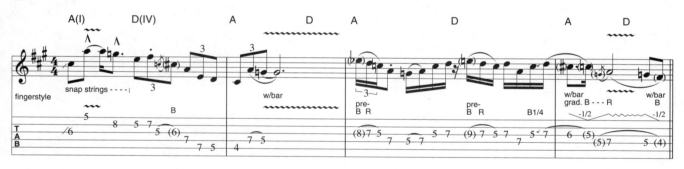

Example 72 — The first two bars of Ex. 72 feature a rhythmic and melodic variation of the previous lick transposed one octave higher to utilize the combined 17th-position *A* pentatonic major and *A* pentatonic minor boxes. Here, our target is an anticipated *F#*, the 3 of the *D* (IV) chord. The 3/16 hemiola in bar 3 uses quarter-bent *C*'s and twin *A*'s to create the illusion of bottleneck slide guitar. Break out of this pattern with a hammer-on into the 3–5–root arpeggio (*C#–E–A*) in bar 4, then slide into the 22nd-fret *B*-string staccato overbend on beat *two*. And don't worry—pain is good! (Hint: For best results, keep those quarter-step bends in constant motion rather than playing them directly on the beat.)

Ex. 72

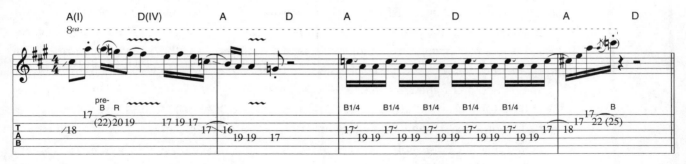

Example 73 — The hybrid-picked 32nd-note trills in Ex. 73 are played on adjacent strings and outline *A7* (with *A* and *G*), *D7sus4* (with *C*, *G*, and *A*), and *A7* (with *C♯*, *G*, and *A*) on the 1st and 2nd strings. The notes that change occur on the 1st string on the downbeats of beats *one* and *three*; otherwise, the flow of alternating 32nd-notes remains constant.

Ex. 73

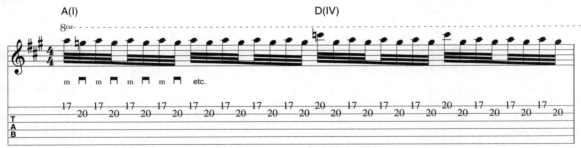

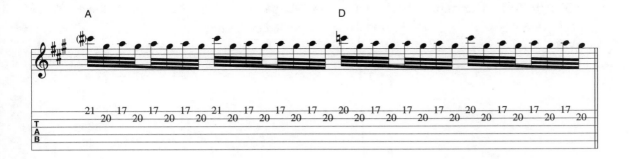

Example 74 — Back in fifth position, Ex. 74 paraphrases our previous pair of licks. Slide into the *A* on beat *one*, add vibrato immediately, cut off the following octave *A* sharply, and then prebend to the same pitch from *G* on the 2nd string and gradually release. The remainder of the measure syncopates a 4–5–♭3–root maneuver that functions as the root–9–♭7–5 of the IV chord. After resting for three-quarters of bar 2, resume with the staccato 16th-note double-stops in bars 3 and 4. We're using the *♭7* and *♯9* (*G* and *C*) of the *A* chord and the 3 and ♭7 (*F♯* and *C*) of the *D* chord to imply *A7♯9* and *D7* tonalities. (Hint: These double-stops can be easily adapted to Beck's signature hybrid-picked adjacent-string trilling technique. Simply claw the *C* on the 1st string with your middle finger, then rapidly alternate 32nd-notes between that note and the picked *G*'s and *F♯*'s on the 2nd string.)

Ex. 74

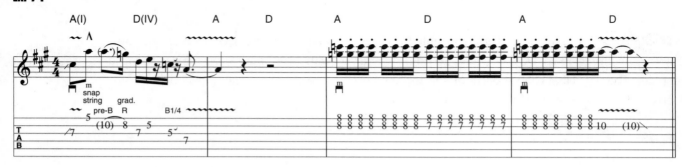

Example 75 — Typically choppy phrasing characterizes the pickup into Ex. 75. Bar 1 begins with two prebends followed by a grace-note bend. Embellished with vibrato, each bend targets the same *A* note. Bend the last 16th-note in bar 1, release it a half-step on the downbeat of bar 2, then rebend, release, and pull off as indicated. Play the *C–C–B–A* 16th-note motif in bar 3 four times, and then convert it to a 3/16 hemiola in bar 4 by trimming off the first *C*. Here we use the same slide move from bar 3 on the first 3/16 grouping, but we replace it with a half-step bend and release for the next three repeats. Wrap it up with a gradual, lazy take on the same bend, sans release.

Ex. 75

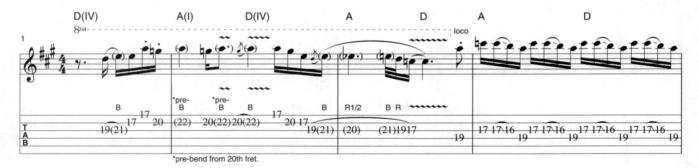

*pre-bend from 20th fret.

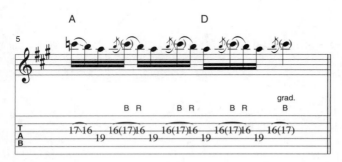

Example 76 — Play Ex. 76 over a swung-16th reggae accompaniment. This lick disproves any notion that Beck's style is all flash and trickery—except for a single slide and pair of teensy quarter-step bends, there's not an ornament in sight. Rake your pick across the 16th-note triplet (see that *A* arpeggio?) on beat *two*, and slide the last note down a half-step to the ♭5 (*E♭*). Continue descending the *A* pentatonic minor scale through beat *three*, then step outside the scale to nail the essence of the IV chord (*D*) with *F♯* on beat *four*. The sequence of ascending 16th-note triplets in bar 2 blends *A* pentatonic major, *A* pentatonic minor, and *A* blues scale elements into a jazz-tinged treat for the ears. Try playing this one with a fairly clean tone.

Ex. 76

Groove #7

Up-tempo 4/4 fusion boogie with fast 12/8 feel.

Key: *G*   **Tempo**: ♩ = 112–130

Suggested accompaniment: Another repetitive vamp, this time on a single I chord (*G5*). This one's a no-brainer. Simply pump out an unbroken string of *G5* swung eighths using the illustrated voicing and rhythm. Use palm muting to keep those staccato downbeats short and sweet.

Tips: You can add harmonic motion to this static vamp with the following *G5–F/G* chord voicings and rhythm figure, or have your bassist provide a steady *G* root while you explore the illustrated *G–F* triad inversions.

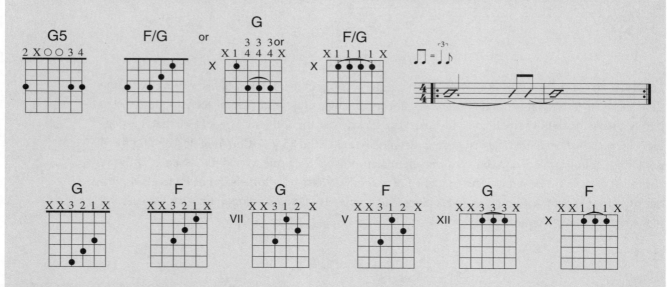

Recommended listening: "Freeway Jam" on *Jeff Beck with the Jan Hammer Group Live* (Epic).

Example 77 — The 15th-position moves in Ex. 77 reveal Beck's early infatuation with a seminal jazz-rock fusion unit, the Mahavishnu Orchestra, and, particularly, the band's keyboard player, synth pioneer Jan Hammer (who eventually became Beck's bandmate and close collaborator). In true call-and-response tradition, the first two eighth-note triplets in bars 1 and 2 are identical—an ascending 5–♭7–root run plus a ♭7–root grace hammer followed by the ♭7 and root. In the first measure, beats *two* and *three* are also identical. This opening motif concludes with a staccato bend to the 5 on beat *four*. Pure Jan Hammer, the two-against-three lick in the second half of bar 2 is a nice reminder that not all string bends need to be relegated to the *G*, *B*, and high-*E* strings. Repeat bars 1 and 2 to complete the lick.

Ex. 77

Example 78 — Another two-bar string of eighth-note triplets, Ex. 78 begins with a series of broken minor 3rds traveling up the *G* and *B* strings to a different position on each beat. The fret-position landmarks for your 1st finger are as follows: In bar 1, beat *one* is in third position, beat *two* is in sixth position, beat *three* is in eighth position, and beat *four* is in 11th position. In bar 2, beat *one* is in 13th position and beat *two* is in 15th position. The descending grace slides on beats *three* and *four* in bar 2—again played using two-against-three phrasing—emit a distinct bottleneck aroma.

Ex. 78

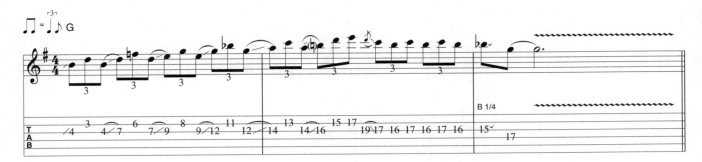

Example 79 — The trickery in Ex. 79 involves open-*G*-string pull-offs—originating from *B♭* (the #9) 15 frets higher—and whole-step whammy-bar dips to *F* (the ♭7). The rhythmic feel of this lick shifts from swung eighths in bars 1 and 2 to quarter-note triplets in bars 3 and 4.

Ex. 79

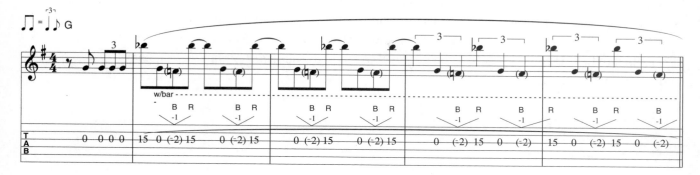

Example 80, our last boogie with Beck, begins with cool start-and-stop phrasing as we navigate hairpin turns through the 15th-position *G* pentatonic minor box. Hold the slightly delayed bend in bar 3 until its release on beat *three* of bar 4. Follow up with the descending triplet lead-in to bar 5, where we nail the ♭7 (*F*) before prebending it up to the root. (Don't forget to add vibrato.) The concluding phrase in bars 6 and 7 summarizes our study of Beck-style licks quite nicely. Following the initial ♭3–3 hammer-on, 5, and root, a two-note pentatonic minor sequence begins to emerge starting on beat *two*, but, instead of continuing it, we briefly slide out of 15th position to the 14th-fret *A* and then return for a root–♭7–5 triplet and final ♭7–root grace-note hammer-on. Mm-mm good!

Ex. 80

JIMMY PAGE

NLIKE HIS BROTHER YARDBIRDS, Jimmy Page had to be lured away from a successful and prestigious career as a studio musician to join the band. Working alongside UK studio giants like Big Jim Sullivan, young Page had already lent his impressive guitar skills to recording artists from the Who and the Kinks to Donovan and Screaming Lord Sutch. When he finally relented and joined the band, Page brought a wealth of new musical ideas, many of which would be developed into blueprints for his next project. Following stints with and without Jeff Beck, Page finally quit the band in 1968, taking its name with him. His New Yardbirds soon evolved into Led Zeppelin, and the rest, as they say, is history.

When both bands emerged at nearly the same time, it seemed as if the Jeff Beck Group and Led Zeppelin were in fierce competition to claim the throne left vacant by Cream's demise. This was reinforced by the fact that both bands covered Willie Dixon's "You Shook Me" on their first albums, and both were guitar-led power trios with flamboyant lead singers. But, in truth, they were as different as apples and oranges. Though the blues connection was obvious, Page's affection for Celtic folk stylings was woven deeply into the fabric of Led Zeppelin. And, unlike Beck, Page proved to be a visionary producer and adept orchestrator—a master of mic placement and over-dubbed guitar armadas. Need it be said that the entire Zeppelin catalog remains compulsory listening for guitarists of all ages and creeds?

Since the collapse of Led Zeppelin following drummer John Bonham's untimely death in 1980, Page's output has been somewhat spotty but memorable, with several solo and group efforts (including *Outrider* and *The Firm*), plus various reunions with Zep vocalist Robert Plant and bassist John Paul Jones and a guest spot with the Black Crowes.

Primarily known as a Gibson Les Paul player, Page actually used a Fender Telecaster through a small Supro amp to record many Zeppelin classics, including "Communication Breakdown" and the guitar solo on "Stairway to Heaven." Gibson eventually produced a Jimmy Page model Les Paul (equipped with an onboard servo-controlled automatic tuning system, no less!), but the pragmatic guitar wizard has always vacillated among Les Pauls, Danelectros, Stratocasters, and Teles, including one routed for a Parsons *B*-string bender. Page was another early Marshall devotee, but he also sported the cleanest sound of the bunch—almost like the biggest, loudest acoustic guitar you ever heard. Overall, Page's lead playing has a nervous, edgy quality that often seems to teeter on the brink of chaos. Cool—that works for me!

Our 21 Page-style licks come grouped in five accompaniment grooves. Have at them and rock on!

JIMMY PAGE–Style Licks

Groove #1
Heavy rock with fast eighth-note feel.

Key: *E*   **Tempo:** ♩ = 154–174

Suggested accompaniment: For Examples 81 and 82, alternate measures of *E5* eighth-notes with a bar of *D–A–D* chords—played on the "and" of beat *one,* and then beats *three* and *four.* (Note: There is no accompaniment for Examples 83a and 83b.)

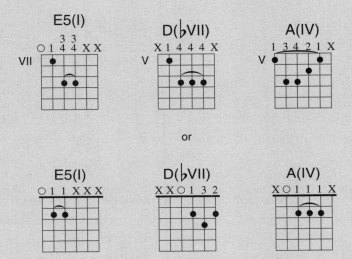

or

Tips: Led Zeppelin had a tendency to deconstruct song grooves on the fly during their extended live performances. It wasn't unusual for a pumped-up eighth-note rock groove to suddenly morph into a funky half-time figure in mid-song, as in Examples 83a and 83b.

Recommended listening: Led Zeppelin, "Communication Breakdown" on *Led Zeppelin* (Atlantic) and various Led Zeppelin compilations.

Example 81 — The basic move that opens Ex. 81 may look familiar, but its phrasing and rhythm separate it from similar Clapton- and Beck-style licks. Anchor your fret hand in 12th position and gradually stretch the 4 (*A*) up to the 5 (*B*) using an even bending motion that begins as soon as you pick the *A* and peaks on *B* a half-beat later. Follow up with the high-*E* root and ♭7–5 (*D–B*) pull-off on beat *two*, then repeat the entire two-beat motif three times. The third measure starts with the same bend but quickly morphs into a descending *E* pentatonic minor–based sequence of eighth-note triplets that span two measures. On beat *four* of bar 3, the sequence briefly deviates from its mathematical order to avoid predictability—way cool.

Ex. 81

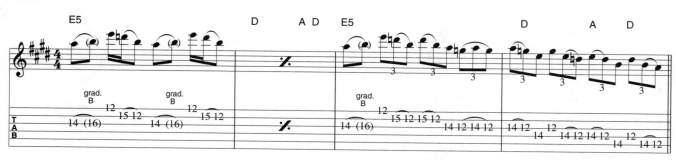

Example 82 — Retain the same triplet feel and remain in 12th position for the first two measures of Ex. 82. Check out how bars 1 and 2—the "call" portion of the lick—feature identical eighth-note triplets on beats *one* and *two*, while repeated notes are added to and then subtracted from the bends on beats *two* and *four*. In bar 1 you'll find a single quarter-note on beat *two* and two eighth-notes on beat *four*. On the second beat of bar 2, we add a third note to form an eighth-note triplet before reverting back to a pair of eighths on beat *four*. This additive/subtractive style of rhythmic phrasing can make it appear as though the lick is speeding up and slowing down. In bars 3 and 4—the "response" portion of the lick—we slip up to 15th position for a quick run of eighths followed by a trio of syncopated bends to the 5 (*B*). Release the last of these on the downbeat of bar 4 and finish with a pair of adjacent whole- and half-step bends.

Ex. 82

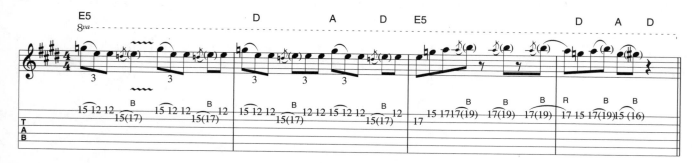

Example 83a — Originating from the previous fast-eighth groove, the following pair of repetitive riffs illustrates the type of half-time funky breakdowns that Led Zeppelin often incorporated into their extended live jams. (Note: These two examples are notated at the same tempo as the original groove; the snare drum backbeats now fall on beat *three* of each measure.)

The hybrid-picked bass figure in Ex. 83a reveals Page's predilection for funky, James Brown–style R&B riffs. Following its opening broken *E* octaves, bar 1 utilizes contrary motion between the *E* and *D* strings to imply *G* and *D* chord sounds. The hammer–pull maneuver in bar 2 creates a momentary *D–Dsus4–D* flavor, and the *A–E* slide on beat *four* sets you up for the *D–E* hammer-on and reprised *E* octaves in bar 3. Answer this musical query with the double-stops in bar 4; the first hit is syncopated and the last two fall squarely on beats *three* and *four*. In this case, the "call" portion of the lick occupies three measures, while the "response" lasts for only one. Think of it as a 75/25 split versus 50/50.

Ex. 83a

Example 83b takes another funky JB groove and whips it into a frenzy drenched with rock 'n' roll attitude and swagger. Though more repetitious than our previous example—bars 1–3 are identical—both share the "75/25 split" concept. Additionally, the double-stop pull-offs in bar 4 introduce a brief three-against-two hemiola before the figure repeats.

Ex. 83b

Groove #2 Heavier rock with faster eighth-note feel.

Key: *E*   **Tempo:** ♩ = 160–185

Suggested accompaniment: A repetitive ascending and descending *E* pentatonic minor bass line. Play 4–5–♭7–root–♭3–4–♭3–root (*A–B–D–E–G–A–G–E*) as a steady stream of eighth-notes, but omit the last root (*E*) in every other measure.

E bass riff

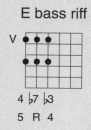

4 ♭7 ♭3
5 R 4

Tips: Another demonstration of the Led Zep jam machine in action, this groove began with a slow, spooky 12/8 vibe before it was transformed into a screaming 4/4 blues-rock rave-up. You could easily interchange any of these licks with those from our previous groove.

Recommended listening: Led Zeppelin, "Dazed and Confused" on *Led Zeppelin* (Atlantic) and various Led Zeppelin compilations.

Example 84 — The syncopated eighth-notes at the beginning of the first three bars of Ex. 84 create a stuttering start/stop effect that is atypical of Page's style. Following an initial quarter-step bend on the pickup, the *G*'s on the "and" of beat *four* in bars 1 and 2 are bent a whole-step to *A*. Another "75/25 split" played in 12th position, the lick concludes in bar 4 via an ascending *E* pentatonic minor run decorated with chromatic passing tones and a 4–♭3 (*A–G*) pull-off.

Ex. 84

Example 85 begins with a repetitive 16th–16th–eighth/♭3–root–♭7 motif (*G–E–D*) played for seven beats. Bar 3 reveals the logic behind positioning ourselves at the 17th fret rather than the 12th; we're now in perfect position for the concluding run in bars 3 and 4—a signature Page-ism that blends *E* pentatonic major and *E* blues scale elements for a quasi-country vibe.

Ex. 85

Example 86 slows down the pace and exhibits a bit more harmonic sophistication than your average rock 'n' roll lick. Examine the repetitive 3/8 hemiola motif and you'll find that it forms a reverse *D* major arpeggio (*A–F#–D*)—a standard substitution in jazz. Analyze these tones against the *E* root and you'll discover that they function as its 11, 9, and ♭7—all very hip-sounding upper extensions of the tonic *E* triad. In bar 2, we begin a descending three-note melodic sequence that redefines our *D* arpeggio as *Gmaj7*, thus creating an *Em9* tonality.

Cool Substitution Rules: Arpeggiating a major triad one whole-step below a key center gives you the ♭7, 9, and 11 of that key. A major-7 arpeggio played a minor 3rd (three half-steps) higher than the key center produces a minor-9th sound over the tonic.

Ex. 86

Example 87 — We've displaced and elongated the trademark Page move from Ex. 85 to cover the first bar-and-a-half of Ex. 87. (Tip: Try playing this six-note motif as a repetitious 6/8 hemiola displaced over several measures.) The repetitive rhythmic motif that follows pedals *E*'s and *D*'s on the *B* string with a series of descending bends—5–6 (*B–C♯*), ♭3–4 (*G–A*), root–2 (*E–F♯*) and ♭7–root (*D–E*)—before concluding with a trio of *G*'s.

Ex. 87

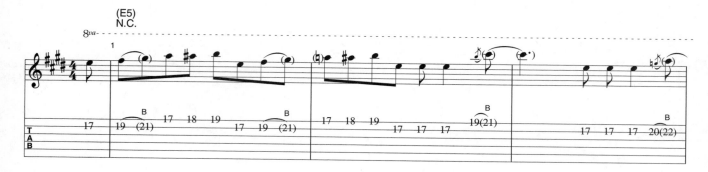

Example 88 — Our last lick played over this groove, Ex. 88 features the surprisingly advanced usage of arpeggiated three-note major triads ascending in ♭5 intervals over implied IV and V chords (*B* and *A*). But don't worry—it's actually much easier than it sounds. Dig this: The first three notes form an ascending *B* major arpeggio, and the next three notes form an ascending *F* major arpeggio. These are located a ♭5 (three whole-steps) apart and utilize the same three-note shape. Both are repeated one octave higher (be sure to raise the notes on the *B* string a half-step), and then capped with an additional *B* arpeggio played another octave higher. Next, the entire two-bar figure is transposed a whole-step lower to cover the *A* chord in bars 3 and 4. We finish with a very Hendrix-y bounce between the low *E* string and *E7#9* chord punctuations.

Ex. 88

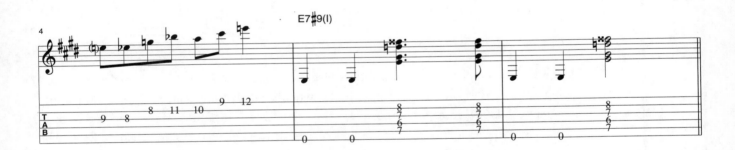

Groove #3

Proto-metal with 16th-note feel.

Key: *F#*   **Tempo:** ♩= 92–112

Suggested accompaniment: A galloping bass figure that lays on the root (*F#*) with snare-synced octave punctuations on beats *two* and *four*. This two-beat rhythmic motif is played twice to complete the measure.

F# octaves

R   oct

Tips: Drop this *C9*—the ♭V chord—into the single-note riff as an accented quarter-note on beat *four*.

C9

Recommended listening: Led Zeppelin, "Immigrant Song" on *Led Zeppelin III* and *How the West Was Won* (both on Atlantic).

Example 89 — The emphasis on a 16th-note pulse in this moderately fast groove makes it perfect for ripping 16th-note triplets or scratching funky syncopated rhythms. Played over a thundering heavy-metal beat, Ex. 89 recasts the repetitive four-note lick from Ex. 81 a whole-step higher as a grace-bent eighth-note followed by a 16th-note triplet. Now played within a single beat, this rounded-off rhythmic motif literally flies off your fingertips once you get in the zone. Though the lick is only shown for one measure, you can keep it going as long as you like before segueing to the rapid-fire blur of 16th-note triplets in bar 2.

Ex. 89

Example 90 — Funky syncopations abound in Ex. 90, another "75/25 split" call-and-response lick. The "question"—established in bar 1—scratches 16th- and 14th-fret double-stops on the *G* and *B* strings. Play it three times, but cut the third repeat short, as indicated. Anticipate bar 4 by sliding into the sixth-fret *G#* with your 3rd finger. This aligns your fret-hand index finger in the fourth position— precisely where you want to be for the 2nd-finger hammer-on and pinky pull-off in the first half of that measure. Look closely and you'll see the same substitution we used back in Ex. 86, though this version is slightly embellished and transposed to *F#*. In this case, we're layering a slippery *Emaj7* arpeggio over the *F#* chord. The additional extension (*D#*) functions as the 6, or 13, of *F#*, lending an even greater air of sophistication to the proceedings. We wrap it up with a silky index-finger slide into second position for a descending *F#* blues scale—literally!

Cool New Substitution Rule: Playing a major-7th arpeggio a whole-step lower than a major or minor chord produces ♭7, 9, 11, and 13 extensions.

Ex. 90

Example 91 illustrates how Page could stretch a simple idea over several measures and still keep it interesting. Built from just three fretted notes (*F#*, *E*, and *A*), this lick evolves from a combination of eighth-notes and syncopated 16th-notes (bars 1 and 2) to a steady stream of 16ths, conveniently grouped in fours (bars 3 and 4). Learn the rhythm in bar 1 first and you'll have most of bar 2 wired. Catch the pickup on the "and" of beat *four* and it's off to the races—just be careful not to rush those bends.

Ex. 91

Groove #4

Slow 12/8 minor blues.

Key: *C minor*   **Tempo:** ♩ = 40–44

Suggested accompaniment: 12-bar quick-change minor blues progression with Im, IVm, and Vm chords (*Cm*, *Fm*, and *Gm*). For these examples, play sustained *Cm* and *Fm* chords as either dotted whole-notes or dotted half-notes, or a mixture of both.

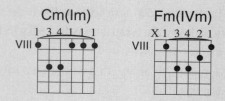

Tips: Add variety to your accompaniment by playing dotted quarter-notes, then cut every other one short with staccato phrasing. And remember, you can approach any chord from a half-step above or below.

Recommended listening: Led Zeppelin, "Since I've Been Loving You" on Led *Zeppelin III* (Atlantic) and various Led Zeppelin compilations.

Example 92 — There's a lot of music crammed into the next two examples, so let's break them down into bite-sized pieces by treating each 3/8 dotted-quarter beat as a separate event. In Ex. 92, the pickup and first half of bar 1 are straightforward enough—an eighth-note slide into the 5 (*G*) is followed by a root–b7–5 triplet (*C–Bb–G*) and subsequent dotted-half-note grace bend to the root. This move anchors us in eighth position, where we remain for the entire lick. From here on, it's a bit of a roller-coaster ride. Counting each beat *one*–"and"–*two*–"and"–*three*–"and," wait for the second 16th of beat *three* to nail the *F–G* bend, and then follow it with a 16th-note triplet and quick 32nd-note hammer-on. This leads to another 16th-note triplet on beat *four* (with its first note tied) followed by four ascending 16ths. The last note in bar 2 (*Ab*) is borrowed from the *C* natural minor scale (also known as *C* Aeolian mode) to anticipate the change to the IVm chord (*Fm*) in bar 2—*Ab* is the b3 of *Fm*.

We begin bar 2 by playing a reverse *Ab* major arpeggio (*Eb–C–Ab*) on the first, second, and sixth 16th-notes of beat *one* to create an *Fm7* sound. View beat *one* in tandem with beat *two*, and an *Fm9* comes into focus. Learn the rhythm as two 16th-notes, a 16th-note triplet, and two more 16ths before adding the rhythmic tie between the second and third notes. Beat *three* is divided straight down the middle—the first note gets the first three 16ths and the last three notes get the remaining three. Bend into beat *four* for two consecutive pairs of 16ths, then flutter that 32nd-note triplet hammer-on/pull-off combo to the root and b3. Hammer-on the 4 on the downbeat of bar 3 and wrap up the return to the Im chord with a classic B.B. King "dee–da–da" lick. Play Ex. 92 over bars 1–3 of a 12-bar *C* minor blues progression.

Ex. 92

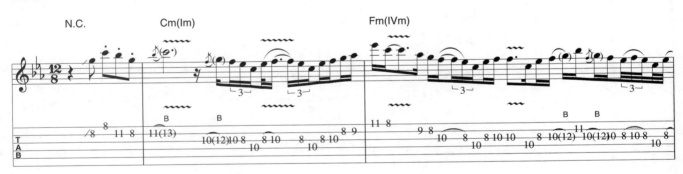

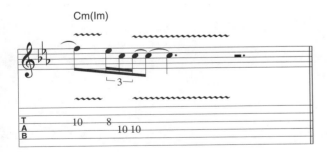

Example 93 navigates the IVm–Im (*Fm–Cm*) change found in bars 5–7 in a 12-bar *C* minor blues progression with a cool move that relocates us to the 13th position. This jazzy pickup anticipates the impending *Fm* chord by a full dotted-quarter beat. Use your 3rd finger and pinky to play the opening three notes, and then barre your index finger across the top three strings to form an *Fm* triad at the 13th fret and rake the 32nd-note triplet in reverse with a smooth upstroke. Immediately slur the last note of this triplet down a half-step from *A♭* to *G*, then tag on the *F* root another whole-step lower. You can analyze these notes as the *F* Dorian mode minus its 6, *F* pentatonic minor plus its 9, or simply as an *Fm9* arpeggio. Whatever you call it, it's a common move in jazz, but practically unheard of in rock 'n' roll.

On beat *one* of bar 1, you'll find a pair of 16th-note triplets that dance around the 9 (*G*) with *F* pentatonic minor tones, and an anticipated root that ties into beat *two*. The second beat closes with a pair of swung 16ths that serve as a pickup to the beat-long bend on beat *three*. Beat *four* houses a tricky but vital rhythm—a 16th-note, an eighth-note, and another 16th tied to the first note of a 16th-note triplet—plus a whopping two-step bend!

Bar 2 begins with another pair of swung 16ths followed by a vibrated quarter-note—a quivering quaver, if you will. An eighth-rest on beat *two* provides a quick breather before we slide back to the eighth-position *C* pentatonic minor box and bend-and-choke into beat *three*. The adjacent 16th-note triplets that follow descend the *C* pentatonic minor scale alphabetically. Beat *four* utilizes an eighth-note and four 16ths to lead us back to the Im (*Cm*) for three consecutive 16th-note triplets and a dip in and out of sixth position.

Ex. 93

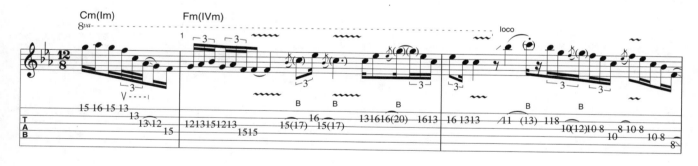

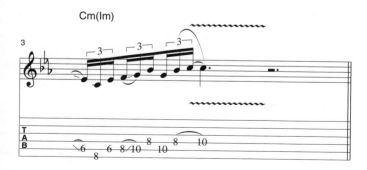

Groove #5

Anthemic arena rock
with eighth-note feel.

Suggested accompaniment: Classic Im–♭VII–♭VI (*Am–G–F*) progression. Create a repetitive two-bar rhythm figure by playing the first two chords as half-notes and the third as a whole-note.

Am(Im)

G(♭VII)

F(♭VI)

Tips: You'll hear alternate versions of a few familiar if not historic riffs in these examples. For variety, play *Am* and *G* as eighth-notes, but rest for all of beats *two* and *four* and then anticipate the whole-note *F* chord on the "and" of beat *four*.

Recommended listening: Led Zeppelin, "Stairway to Heaven" on *Led Zeppelin IV* (Atlantic) and various Led Zeppelin compilations.

These two-bar licks recall some of the greatest moments in what we now call classic rock. The once new-sounding Im–♭VII–♭VI (*Am–G–F*) progression that fueled magical and mystical excursions such as Zeppelin's "Stairway to Heaven" and Hendrix's take on Dylan's "All Along the Watchtower" has been all but worn out by years of banal abuse. Let's return for a moment to a time of grandeur and revisit these variations on some classic Page licks that are still echoing in the cosmos.

Example 94a and 94b — Ex. 94a begins with a third-finger slide that situates your fret hand in the fifth-position *A* pentatonic minor box—the source of this lick except for its very last note. This ♭6 (*F*) introduces an *A* Aeolian, or natural minor, element that coincides perfectly with the ♭VI chord (*F*).

The pickup to Ex. 94b consists of a third-finger ♭7–root (*G–A*) bend followed by a pair of ♭3 (*C*) eighth-notes. Dig in to the ♭3–4 (*C–D*) bend on beat *one*, milk the ♭3 and root (*C* and *A*), and then slide up to the 10th fret to lock into eighth position for the remainder of the lick. The run over the *F* chord is strictly pentatonic minor, but you could easily sub *F* for the *E* on the last 16th of beat *one*.

Ex. 94a

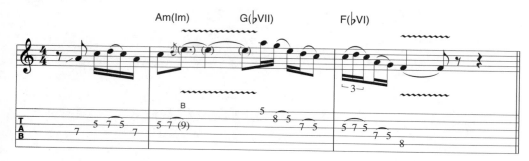

Ex. 94b

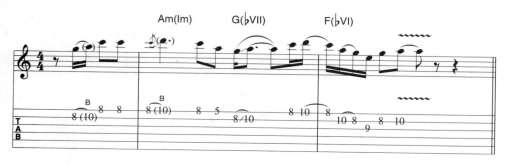

Example 95 — The only interruptions in the steady flow of 16th-notes in Ex. 95 are a shortly sustained ♭3 (C) and a momentary 16th-rest in bar 1. We've seen these pentatonic moves before, but the mid-measure shift to the ♭VII chord (G) recasts them in a new light. Bar 2 begins with a slide from G to a trio of F 16ths that coincide with the ♭VI chord (F). The last three 16ths in beat *two* form an ascending F major arpeggio, and the measure concludes with two beats of *A* pentatonic minor action played in both the fifth and eighth positions.

Ex. 95

Example 96 — We're back in eighth position for the pickup to Ex. 96. This five-note fragment begins on the last 16th-note of beat *three* and targets the ♭3 (C) on the downbeat of bar 1. The *A–B* grace-bend sounds very, well, graceful—after all, *B* is the 3 of the ♭VII chord (G). Rhythmically, bar 1 jumps from quarter-notes to eighths to syncopated 16ths in a herky-jerky fashion typical of the Page style. Stay in eighth position and bend the *G* to *A* using your index finger, or get a head start on the pending shift to fifth position by bending it with your 3rd finger—the choice is yours.

Ex. 96

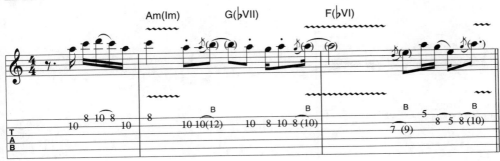

Example 97 — The pickup and opening run in Ex. 97 transport us back to EC territory, but the bendy syncopations and barrage of 16th-notes that follow recall Page at his fieriest. Use the rest on beat *three* to reorient your fret hand in the 13th position, and have at it. The final bend in bar 2 kicks off a repetitive motif composed of the previous five notes. You can play this 3/8 hemiola over as many cycles of the chord progression as you see fit.

Ex. 97

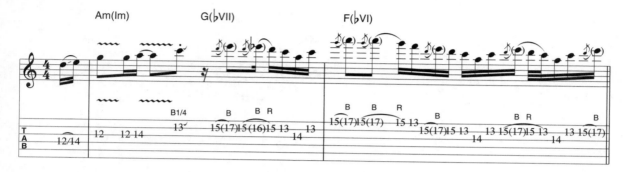

Example 98a — Our final pair of licks—Page-style or otherwise—show how ideas can be developed from one lick to the next. (By this time, I'm sure you've grasped the idea that many of the licks in this book can be strung together or mixed and matched to form longer lines.) The staccato-16th pickup and first four notes of beat *one* in Ex. 98a outline a 3/8 hemiola that repeats three times over the course of bar 1. Bar 2 begins with Hendrix-influenced obliquely hammered double-stops and ends with a pair of double-hammered 16th-note triplets that plant the seed for our last example.

Ex. 98a

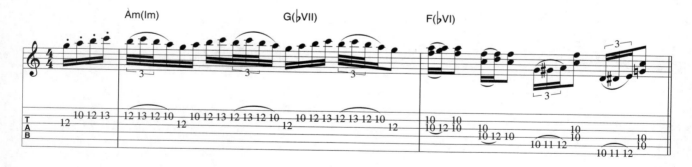

Example 98b — You can see the roots of Ex. 98b take shape during the last two beats of Ex. 98a, only here the 16th-note stays put, acting as a three-note pedal against the shifting *C, D, F,* and *G* eighth-note upbeats. Extend this lick by continuing the pedal and playing different *A* minor scale tones on the offbeat eighths.

Ex. 98b

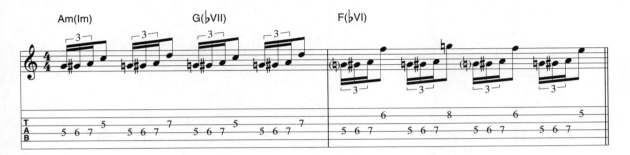

Well, that does it. Hopefully, this collection will light your fire as much as it did mine. Remember, all tech-talk aside, these licks are all about feel and emotion—you'll get as much out of them as you put into them. It ain't easy, but the rewards certainly are sweet. What's that? Your fingers hurt? Now you're talking! See you in the next Guitar Lick Factory!

APPENDIX

Scales and Modes

Many of the licks in *Guitar Licks of the Brit-Rock Heroes* were derived from the following scales and modes:

ERIC CLAPTON–Style Licks

Clapton Groove #1

G pentatonic minor: *G–B♭–C–D–F*
G blues: *G–B♭–C–D♭–D–F*
G pentatonic major: *G–A–B–D–E*

Clapton Groove #2

A pentatonic major: *A–B–C#–E–F#*
A pentatonic minor: *A–C–D–E–G*

Clapton Groove #3

D pentatonic minor: *D–F–G–A–C*

Clapton Groove #4

A pentatonic minor: see Groove #2
A pentatonic major: see Groove #2

Clapton Groove #5

A pentatonic minor: see Groove #2
A pentatonic major: see Groove #2

Clapton Groove #6

C pentatonic minor: *C–E♭–F–G–B♭*
C blues: *C–E♭–F–G♭–G–B♭*
C pentatonic major: *C–D–E–G–A*

Clapton Groove #7

D pentatonic minor: see Groove #3
D Dorian: *D–E–F–G–A–B–C*

JEFF BECK–Style Licks

Beck Groove #1
G pentatonic major: *G–A–B–D–E*
G pentatonic minor: *G–B♭–C–D–F*
G blues: *G–B♭–C–D♭–D–F*
G Mixolydian: *G–A–B–C–D–E–F*
G Dorian: *G–A–B♭–C–D–E–F*

Beck Groove #2
B pentatonic minor: *B–D–E–F♯–A*
B blues: *B–D–E–F–F♯–A*
B pentatonic major: *B–C♯–D♯–F♯–G♯*
B Mixolydian: *B–C♯–D♯–E–F♯–G♯–A*
B Dorian: *B–C♯–D–E–F♯–G♯–A*

Beck Groove #3
F♯ pentatonic minor: *F♯–A–B–C♯–E*
F♯ blues: *F♯–A–B–C–C♯–E*
F♯ pentatonic major: *F♯–G♯–A♯–C♯–D♯*
F♯ Mixolydian: *F♯–G♯–A♯–B–C♯–D♯–E*
F♯ Dorian: *F♯–G♯–A–B–C♯–D♯–E*

Beck Groove #4
G blues: see Groove #1
G pentatonic minor: see Groove #1
G pentatonic major: see Groove #1
G Mixolydian: see Groove #1

Beck Groove #5
G blues: see Groove #1
G pentatonic minor: see Groove #1
G pentatonic major: see Groove #1

Beck Groove #6
A blues: *A–C–D♭–D–E–G*
A Mixolydian: *A–B–C♯–D–E–F♯–G*
A Dorian: *A–B–C–D–E–F♯–G*
A pentatonic minor: *A–C–D–E–G*
A pentatonic major: *A–B–C♯–E–F♯*

Beck Groove #7
G Mixolydian: see Groove #1
G Dorian: see Groove #1
G blues: see Groove #1
G pentatonic minor: see Groove #1
G pentatonic major: see Groove #1

JIMMY PAGE–Style Licks

Page Groove #1

E pentatonic minor: *E–G–A–B–D*

E pentatonic major: *E–F#–G#–B–C#*

Page Groove #2

E pentatonic minor: see Groove #1

E pentatonic major: see Groove #1

E Dorian: *E–F#–G–A–B–C#–D*

Page Groove #3

F# pentatonic minor: *F#–A–B–C#–E*

F# Dorian: *F#–G#–A–B–C#–D#–E*

F# blues: *F#–A–B–C–C#–E*

Page Groove #4

C pentatonic minor: *C–E♭–F–G–B*

C minor [Aeolian]: *C–D–E♭–F–G–A♭–B♭*

Page Groove #5

A pentatonic minor: *A–C–D–E–G*

A minor (Aeolian): *A–B–C–D–E–F–G*

<u>ERIC CLAPTON—Style Licks</u>

Clapton Groove #1

Track 01: Ex. 1
Track 02: Ex. 2
Track 03: Ex. 3
Track 04: Ex. 4
Track 05: Ex. 5
Track 06: Ex. 6
Track 07: Ex. 7
Track 08: Ex. 8
Track 09: Ex. 9
Track 10: Ex. 10
Track 11: Ex. 11
Track 12: Ex. 12
Track 13: Ex. 13
Track 14: Ex. 14
Track 15: Ex. 15
Track 16: Ex. 16
Track 17: Ex. 17

Clapton Groove #2

Track 18: Ex. 18
Track 19: Ex. 19
Track 20: Ex. 20

Clapton Groove #3

Track 21: Ex. 21
Track 22: Ex. 22
Track 23: Ex. 23
Track 24: Ex. 24
Track 25: Ex. 25
Track 26: Ex. 26
Track 27: Ex. 27

Clapton Groove #4

Track 28: Ex. 28
Track 29: Ex. 29
Track 30: Ex. 30
Track 31: Ex. 31
Track 32: Ex. 32
Track 33: Ex. 33
Track 34: Ex. 34

Clapton Groove #5

Track 35: Ex. 35
Track 36: Ex. 36

Clapton Groove #6

Track 37: Ex. 37

Clapton Groove #7

Track 38: Ex. 38
Track 39: Ex. 39
Track 40: Ex. 40

JEFF BECK—Style Licks

Beck Groove #1
Track 41: Ex. 41a & 41b
Track 42: Ex. 42a & 42b
Track 43: Ex. 43a & 43b
Track 44: Ex. 44a & 44b
Track 45: Ex. 45a & 45b
Track 46: Ex. 46a & 46b
Track 47: Ex. 47a & 47b
Track 48: Ex. 48a & 48b

Beck Groove #2
Track 49: Ex. 49
Track 50: Ex. 50
Track 51: Ex. 51
Track 52: Ex. 52
Track 53: Ex. 53
Track 54: Ex. 54
Track 55: Ex. 55
Track 56: Ex. 56

Beck Groove #3
Track 57: Ex. 57a & 57b
Track 58: Ex. 58
Track 59: Ex. 59
Track 60: Ex. 60
Track 61: Ex. 61a & 61b
Track 62: Ex. 62
Track 63: Ex. 63

Beck Groove #4
Track 64: Ex. 64
Track 65: Ex. 65
Track 66: Ex. 66

Beck Groove #5
Track 67: Ex. 67
Track 68: Ex. 68
Track 69: Ex. 69
Track 70: Ex. 70

Beck Groove #6
Track 71: Ex. 71
Track 72: Ex. 72
Track 73: Ex. 73
Track 74: Ex. 74
Track 75: Ex. 75
Track 76: Ex. 76

Beck Groove #7
Track 77: Ex. 77
Track 78: Ex. 78
Track 79: Ex. 79
Track 80: Ex. 80

JIMMY PAGE–Style Licks

Page Groove #1
Track 81: Ex. 81
Track 82: Ex. 82
Track 83: Ex. 83a & 83b

Page Groove #2
Track 84: Ex. 84
Track 85: Ex. 85
Track 86: Ex. 86
Track 87: Ex. 87
Track 88: Ex. 88

Page Groove #3
Track 89: Ex. 89
Track 90: Ex. 90
Track 91: Ex. 91

Page Groove #4
Track 92: Ex. 92
Track 93: Ex. 93

Page Groove #5
Track 94: Ex. 94a & 94b
Track 95: Ex. 95
Track 96: Ex. 96
Track 97: Ex. 97
Track 98: Ex. 98a & 98b
Track 99: **Tune up**

Produced, engineered, and performed by JG at Jesilu Music, Woodstock, New York.

All licks were performed live using a 1962 Gibson Les Paul/SG ebony-block model and 1991 Fender Custom Shop "swirly" Stratocaster with Jeff Beck neck and body by Gary Brawer, through Line 6's GuitarPort.

acknowledgments

THANKS TO Richard Johnston, Nancy Tabor, Matt Kelsey, Kevin Becketti, and Nina Lesowitz at Backbeat Books, and to Liz and Chris Ledgerwood.

I'd also like to extend my love and gratitude to my wife Mary Lou, daughter Deidre, and my extended Gress, Tresolini, and Arnold families.

Finally, I bow to the royal subjects of this book, who have rocked my world for almost four decades. Long live Clapton, Beck, and Page!

PHOTO CREDITS

Page 1: ©Jeff Mayer/Star File

Page 37: ©Retna

Page 73: ©Chuck Boyd/Redferns/Retna

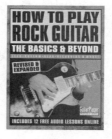